Devon S
of the
Supernatural

Devon Stories of the Supernatural

Judy Chard

COUNTRYSIDE BOOKS
NEWBURY, BERKSHIRE

Designed by Graham Whiteman
Cover design by Peter Davies, Nautilus Design

Produced through MRM Associates Ltd., Reading
Typeset by Mac Style Ltd, Scarborough, N. Yorkshire
Printed by J.W. Arrowsmith Ltd., Bristol

Contents

Foreword

I don't think hauntings just occur, I think some particular physical presence is needed to cause an apparition to appear. Certainly my research has thrown up irrefutable evidence of some kind of powerful physical force which can manifest itself in a number of ways, leaving a lasting impression on those who experience it, such as the story of the lady who stands in a room for the first time, but is overwhelmed by the feeling that she has been there before.

In the 30 years I have spent travelling around Devon giving talks in village halls and broadcasting for both the BBC and commercial stations, such as DevonAir, I have met hundreds of people who brought me their stories, old and new. These people have witnessed goings-on beyond human comprehension, from the banging of doors to the physical manifestation of a figure from the past, to whom, sometimes, they actually speak. Some of them wished to remain anonymous but one thing stood out among the people I interviewed, they had an utter sincerity and belief in what they told me. More often than not this was confirmed either by someone else or by factual evidence from my own research.

In common with others, I think physical violence can leave an imprint on the surroundings through the emotions it releases. Many people feel there are earthbound spirits, which can be benign, or a real danger. Perhaps these spirits are frustrated at not being able to communicate with, or be seen by, the particular occupiers of the house, but there is no doubting that some buildings seem to oppress us with a sense of the people who have lived and died in them. The walls, floors and ceilings are saturated with the exhalations of human emotions.

Then there is the stuff of legend or folklore. At one time, if anyone had told me that a ruined crop was the work of the Devil, that a farmer's cow could be ill-wished or they had seen pixies on Dartmoor I should have fallen about laughing, but not now because I have talked to too many people who have convinced me of such things.

After reading these stories perhaps you too will look twice over your shoulder on some twilit evening as you come down from

Dartmoor, not quite sure if that granite rock really is a stone, or if it moved slightly.

So come with me into the realm of poltergeists and pixies, haunted pubs and castles, and explore the world of witches and tortured lost souls. Finally, take heed of the antics of the Devil, the most evil spirit of all, who spends much of his time in Devon and is merciless in his pursuit of those who cross him.

Enjoy your reading.

Judy Chard

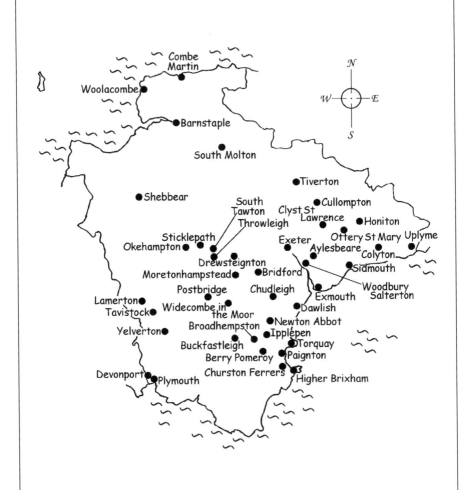

MAP OF DEVON

1

The Ghost of Powderham Castle

The Ghost of Powderham Castle is a friendly ghost, a kind of Florence Nightingale who only appears when a member of the Courtenay family is seriously ill. Gliding along at the top of the castle's grand staircase, she brings hope to sorrowing relatives for they know this means a recovery for the sick member of the family.

At times of stress she has also been seen walking from the castle to Powderham church, which she enters and leaves after a short time. It is thought she works her miracle cure by praying in the church through the night.

Although no one knows for sure who she is, it is believed she is a former Countess of Devon, of which there have been many, for the Courtenays built the Castle in 1390. She is otherwise known as 'the Lady in Grey'.

A governess at the castle claimed to have seen the Lady in Grey twice during the years just after the First World War. She was delighted to see her for Lord Devon, then only two years old, was seriously ill. Soon after the governess's encounters with the ghost, he miraculously recovered.

Venetia, the late Lady Devon, said that what is interesting and important is that all the people who have seen her have been serious, sober people not given to touches of imagination. Nowhere has any word been said against this ghost, in fact records show she has always been welcome, coming as she does at times of crisis.

In a letter to the *Dawlish Gazette,* written in 1975, it was stated that the Lady in Grey was also seen going into the church, in the late 17th century, by a Powderham resident.

In a handwritten letter by Venetia Devon, dated August 1945, she wrote of an occurrence at the outbreak of war in September 1939, which was repeated in a typewritten letter from Lord Courtenay in 1993 to a Miss St Aubyn. She had written to him asking about the hauntings at Powderham.

He writes, 'There is one part of the castle, at the head of the main staircase, which has a distinct feel about it and has been the source of one or two strange happenings. As children we used to have to pass through it on the way to my parents' bedroom and we never did so at a walk! The Grey Lady is known to appear in this area from time to time and has been seen by visitors who are usually unaware that she is not real. I have been told she is inclined to appear when someone in the house is ill but I cannot verify that. I have never met her myself.'

He goes on: 'We have recently taken to doing guided tours of the house and our guides have therefore made us rather more aware of visitors' reaction in this part of the building. It is apparent that a number of visitors do become aware of some sort of presence and there have also been a number of incidences apparently of cameras not working, usually for some reason on Tuesday, but this could of course merely be coincidence.'

He then refers to the handwritten account by Venetia Devon, his mother, which describes an occurrence when his father was away fighting in the Second World War.

'The strangest happening in this area, which is completely verified, occurred at the beginning of the last world war, when it was necessary to go round and blackout the windows in the castle. My mother was alone in the house except for my half sister's French governess. Together they went round to verify the blackout. At the head of the staircase is a window with a pair of shutters, which had been duly shut and they went out into the garden to verify it had been effective. In order to close the

Powderham Castle

shutters they had to remove a box of shells from the windowsill to a nearby table.

'It is not known who opened the shutters in the morning but when my mother went to shut them again in the evening to her amazement she found they were fastened open with screws. Rather mystified by this, my mother contacted the house carpenter who told her that he had screwed them back himself 30 years before because the maid said they were "haunted" and could not be kept open.

'The carpenter's only comment was "There's many a ghost I have laid with a few screws!" On revisiting the window, it was clear to my mother the screws were rusty and had certainly been there some time. There was a roller blind, which would have prevented the shutters closing and which you would think they would have used. But they both clearly remember having shut the shutters and indeed the box of shells was on one side where they had put it. This has never been explained or repeated.'

There is also an account of a bedroom in the servants' quarters of the castle where no one could sleep because every time anyone got into bed the clothes were flung to the floor. In 1800 one of the servants visiting the room actually saw this happen.

On the landing below the servants' quarters, there is a room between two floor levels with a separate staircase leading down to it, which was undiscovered for many years. When it was found and opened it contained the skeleton of a woman and child, but this cannot be verified by Lord Courtenay. He said the story might have been invented by his great uncle for the purpose of frightening his father and sisters.

He also adds that the ghost of the 10th Earl was said to have been seen when his great uncle built the wing of the castle in which there are now offices.

'Forty years ago, when alterations were being made, the 10th Earl was seen by the housekeeper standing watching the workmen. She was quite new at the time and subsequently recognised him from his portrait. She was a perfectly level-headed person and not given to hallucinations and worked for us for a number of years.'

Prince Michael of Greece, cousin of Prince Philip, once visited the castle, during which time he discovered two ghosts. He explained: 'One of a young girl who suffered a tragic love affair, she is very happy and friendly but does not have a nice word to say about a much older ghost who haunts another room in the same tower. This is not so pleasant and I did not really want to talk to her myself.'

The castle's general manager, Tim Faulkner, is delighted that some light is now being shed on the mysterious tales. 'We have had some very strange goings on here over the last few years, for example we may have a camera shy ghost because on Tuesday mornings our visitors quite often find that their cameras will not work in one room but work perfectly when they move to the next.' This bears out Lord Courtenay's remarks.

Finally, I have not ventured to the castle myself recently, but if I did I would be sure to have my camera and a companion, to witness anything untoward.

2

Beware the Cloven Hoof

I refer, of course, to the Devil himself. Make no mistake, he still comes to Devon, as he always has, and who could blame him, as least he has good taste in choosing the most beautiful county in all of England. There are minor irritations he causes, however, such as spitting on the blackberries on the 20th of September so they are no longer fit to eat.

It seems spoiling crops is a bit of a favourite pastime. I don't know whether or not the Devil had a hand in a story I read in the local paper recently, when the barley had been spoiled by the wet weather, but it did remind me of a tale about a chap called Franken, after whom the days of 18th, 19th and 20th of May are named Frankmass.

In 1750, Franken bought up a whole lot of barley because it was cheap, Devonian entrepreneurs like a bargain, but then got cold feet, worried that he wouldn't sell enough beer to cover his expenses as a brewer. Looking, as usual, for an easy touch, the Devil offered to buy Franken's soul and in return he would arrange to blight the apple blossom, just when it is usually at its best, on those three days in May. There would then be no cider apples and everyone would want to drink beer. Believe it or not it is very noticeable that often those three nights are frosty.

Over a century earlier, 'Wicked' Jan Reynolds of Widecombe discovered to his cost that entering into a pact with the Devil leads to nothing but trouble. Jan made a deal with Satan whereby he would be provided with money for drinking and gambling until such time as he should be discovered in Widecombe church, when he would become Satan's prey. Jan thought he was pretty safe because he never intended to go anywhere near the church. Drink, however, one of his weaknesses, took him there in a befuddled state one Sunday during the afternoon service. It was a mistake that was to cost Jan his life, along with others in the church, that fateful day in October 1638.

Indeed, the *Guinness Book of Records* still makes reference to the fact that the worst recorded storm in the UK occurred at Widecombe on 21st of October that year, with sixty two injured and four killed. The storm struck on Sunday afternoon when a service was in progress.

The story goes that learning of Jan's arrival at the church, Satan set out at a gallop for the village, only stopping at the Tavistock Inn at Poundsgate to refresh himself. When he offered money for the drink, the terrified woman innkeeper heard the liquid hiss as it went down his throat and for a moment his black cloak swung back to reveal a cloven hoof. After he left, she found the money in her hand had turned to dried leaves.

The Revd George Lyde was conducting the service in Widecombe church that afternoon, when quite unexpectedly the sky became so dark that the congregation could hardly see each other. Suddenly, the church was lit up with flames as a ball of fire burst through one of the windows and passed down the nave, bringing a strong smell of brimstone. The terrified congregation thought the end of the world had come.

Some extraordinary cases of injury and burning were recorded. For instance, the parson's wife was badly scorched, but her child, seated in the same pew, was unhurt.

One woman who tried to leave was so badly burned she died in the night and a man had his skull fractured so that the brains were scattered, sticking to a pillar in the church. Many who were not killed outright died later as a result of injury. Meanwhile, beams crashed down and stones were shaken from the tower, where a pinnacle collapsed, killing another woman. Some said they had seen a black horse tethered there. A dog

Widecombe church where Jan found himself on that fateful afternoon in 1638

was picked up by the whirlwind and killed as it was dashed against the door.

All this time the Revd Lyde remained in the pulpit, praying until the end. At last Master Ralph Rowse, vintner of the town, stood up saying, 'Neighbours, in the name of God shall we venture out of the church?' Revd Lyde replied, 'It is best to make an end with prayers for it is better to die here than in another place'. Possibly he too thought the end of the world had come.

At the same time, a bowling alley near the church was destroyed, looking as though it had been ploughed up. At Brickstone, near Plymouth, hail stones the size of turkey eggs weighing seven ounces fell. Meanwhile, Satan picked up the drunken Jan from the stone tomb on which he was lying, holding four cards, aces, which had certainly brought him no luck.

Satan vaulted into the saddle with his victim, making his horse fly up into the air, and galloped away. The cards fell from Jan's hands near the Warren Inn and as they reached the ground at Vitifer and Birch Tor they formed into small newtakes, or enclosed fields, which can still be seen today, near where West Webburn rises, and even now resemble the form of cards.

The local schoolmaster at the time, Richard Hill, recorded the whole story of this terrible event and it now hangs on the walls of the church. In the floor a long slab of granite covers the remains of Roger Hill, one of the victims. His widow survived him because she had stayed at home to cook the lunch.

The Devil has made numerous other minor visits to Devon, always with catastrophic results for his hapless victims. One evening a moorland farmer, riding home from Widecombe full of cider, saw the whisht hounds in Wistman's Wood, which they still haunt. The man called out, 'Hi there Old Nick, have a good run – did you kill?' The ghostly figure replied, 'Yes, and here's one of them!' with which he threw a bundle to the farmer. It was the corpse of a small child, his own son.

It is said, 'The deeds of Satan, while going to and fro on earth, invariably reveal him in conflict with man, though he is always careful to hide his real intentions and let it appear as though he desired to help'. On one occasion, however, he met his match when his antagonist was no less a person than King Arthur. Satan climbed a high tor and began to throw quoits at the British king who reciprocated from another hill about a mile away. As the quoits fell they became masses of rock and eventually Satan had to admit defeat, leaving Arthur triumphant. The hill on which the king stood is near the road leading from Moretonhampstead to Bridford, known as Blackingstone, whilst the Devil was on Hel Tor further to the north.

Old Nick has also been known to raise terrifying floods if he is thwarted. One Sunday afternoon in 1628, when the good folk of Okehampton were coming out of church, they were surprised to see the eastern branch of the river Okement, which runs through the town, had risen to an enormous height as it crashed down its course. There hadn't been a drop of rain but the water stank of brimstone, proof enough that the Devil's hand was at work.

His footprints, or other mark, may also be seen on many tors and later I shall recount the famous story of these being found in snow. But for the moment let us look at where the prints have made impressions in solid rock. On Mis Tor his frying pan can be seen, a large dish impressed into the hilltop measuring a yard in diameter, where a passing horseman had smelt him cooking 'risty bacon'. He has even visited Lundy, where he blasted out a fissure known as the Devil's Limekiln. He dumped the surplus rock offshore in the form of Shutter Rock as a trap for mariners. The chasm he created is 370ft deep and 250ft wide at the top, dropping down into two sea caves. To crawl to the edge and peer into its depths is a test for the strongest nerves.

As far as churches are concerned, apart from the terrible storm at Widecombe, he was also known in olden days to interfere with the building, between the 12th and 14th century, of the churches of Brent Tor, Buckfastleigh and Plympton.

The first was meant to be built at the foot of the tor, but the builders had hardly proceeded with their work when arriving one morning they found all the stones they had set up had been removed to the top. Bringing them down, they resumed their work. That night, as the clock struck midnight, one or two men who had hidden below the rock saw a tall dark figure approach the site of the intended church and with one kick of his hoof, level all their work. He proceeded to carry the stones to the top of the hill which he had determined should be the site of the church, where it would be difficult to reach.

After several more similar occurrences, the workmen decided to give in, they were no match for the Devil and so there stands the church on the tor.

The story of Buckfastleigh church is exactly the same except the builders built a long flight of steps, which partly thwarted Satan's plan because it was then easily accessible and at least it reminded the local worshippers of its existence.

I mentioned earlier a famous incident of Satan leaving his imprints in the snow. On the night of Thursday 8th February 1855 heavy snow fell all over the county and when the locals awoke they were filled with dread as they looked from their windows. Large hoof prints were clearly visible, eight to twelve inches apart and four by two inches in size, rather like a footprint made by a donkey with one hoof, and they continued in a straight line over 100 miles, both sides of the Exe estuary. They went up walls and fences, over roofs, through locked gates in town, village and hamlet. Was it a bird, a badger or some strange animal loose from a menagerie perhaps, they asked each other? Those with either elder, rowan or ash trees by their gates were smugly superior for they keep off evil and the footsteps had avoided such places. It was obvious this was the Devil himself. Even the *Illustrated London News* ran the story.

It does not do to tempt Satan, however, even if you are a Bishop. In the 13th century, Bishop Bronescombe of Exeter was travelling from Widecombe to Sourton with his chaplain to whom he complained he was tired and hungry and commented, 'When Jesus was in the wilderness he was offered bread made of stone by the Devil. I doubt if I would have had the strength to refuse.'

At that moment a moor man appeared offering the hungry prelate bread and cheese, with the proviso that in payment the Bishop simply get down from his horse, bow low and call him Master. This seemed a fairly mild request to the starving Bishop and he was about to comply when the chaplain caught sight of a cloven hoof and cried out in horror. The stranger was none other than Satan himself. The Bishop made the sign of the cross and the man vanished. The bread and cheese turned immediately to stones, which can still be seen on the side of Amicombe Hill and the area is still known as Bronescombe's Loaf or Bread and Cheese. Nearby are the Slipper Stones, where the Bishop lost his slippers, presumably in his haste to get away.

In Shebbear stands the stone dropped by the Devil when he was flying through the air in one of his usual tempers. It is known as the Devil's Boulder. Every year, on 5th of November, the men of the village perform the ceremony of 'Turning the Boulder'. First the church bells are rung, then men with crowbars undertake the formidable task of turning the stone over. It is believed that calamity will fall on Shebbear if they fail to perform this feat. Apparently, when the ceremony was discontinued during the First World War the following year was one of disaster for the village and neighbouring farms. The juxtaposition of the stone and the church suggests that probably the stone was there first and that the ceremony has very ancient origins. The bell ringing is to drive away evil spirits. During the Second World War church bells were forbidden and it was noticed that all the harvests during those five years were bad.

Finally, joy spread over Dartmoor one day when it was reported the Devil had died of cold at North Lew. A farmer had pulled his carcase out of a bog, horns and tail complete. The celebrations were short lived, however, when it was discovered it was nothing more than a stag! So mind your back on Dartmoor, you never know when he may be after your soul in a moment of weakness.

3

Pixie-Led

Those who have had contact with the little people, or pixies, and I include myself in that, will know that the experience can leave you feeling totally bewildered, as if in a daze. It is not for nothing that pixies are portrayed as mischievous little creatures, because mischief is exactly what they are all about and being pixie-led or pixilated is just one of the tricks they get up to on the highways and byways of the Devon countryside.

More about the experience of being pixie-led later. First we need to explore the nature of these little creatures and their general habitat. Turning to Eric Hemery's definitive book, *High Dartmoor*, he describes how he was taken by a moor man to Huccaby Cleave and shown Pixies' Wood. He remarked that he found the atmosphere 'wisht', perhaps best translated into modern speak as 'spooky'. When he mentioned this to his young companion, the reply was, 'This is the little people's country, there's places I'm quick to run from and places I'd rather not go'. They both fell silent.

Near the centre of Pixies' Wood is a cavern created in the rock mass by frost, inside are candles, matches, a comb and coins put there by people who wish to appease the pixies. Opposite the mouth stands a large tree on which visitors have carved their names recording their visit, for no track or footpath threads the interior of Pixies' Wood. Eric adds, 'No writer has described this and I would not be able to had I not been guided there by a moorman friend'.

The other great writer on Dartmoor, William Crossing, says of pixies in his *Guide to Dartmoor*, 'The former belief in these little elves is one of the most interesting of Devonshire superstitions but their existence is now regarded by people with more than doubt, they are said to be the souls of unbaptised children who cannot enter heaven, they are often seen dressed in green, sometimes they can be mischievous but often they help the industrious housewife or husbandman. Their favourite haunts are the Pixies' Cave on Sheep's Tor, Piskies' Holt or Wood in Huccaby Cleave and New Bridge on the Dart below Holne Bridge.'

The Pixies' Cave on Sheep's Tor, which Crossing mentions, is a curious place. At one time, the small chamber held two or three people but the rocks have moved slowly forward making it much smaller so it is not advisable to enter; in any case if you do, rumour has it your arms will be seized and you will be drawn down beneath the moor.

Theo Brown was another well-known source of information about pixies. She said, 'They present a difficult problem, what on earth are they? But many people do see them, including my own mother. When camping at Postbridge she encountered a rather melancholy figure dressed in green at the top of Drift Lane, but when she approached it and spoke, it "dissolved into thin air", as she put it.'

Like many others, Theo Brown believes pixies are the ghosts of unbaptised babies who can never enter heaven. Gradually they grow weak and feeble and, to improve their 'stock', the pixies steal healthy human babies, taking them from their cots and leaving the weaklings in their place. In fact, many mothers even tied their babies in their cots to prevent such an occurrence.

There are examples of this baby snatching and the tendency for pixies to be malicious if they are crossed. In the 1930s, one man who suffered from this was a yeoman farmer at Fernworthy where the reservoir now stands. He built his house near some rocks, which were a particular haunt of the pixies and they became very angry at this intrusion. He was the last of his family on the male line and was over the moon when his wife had a baby son, shortly after they had moved into their new house.

One evening when he was out at work on the moor, his wife sat beside the fire listening to the wild weather outside; she felt cosy as she rocked the cradle which held her little son, soon she dozed off.

Suddenly she woke to find the baby had gone, mocking laughter sounded outside in the dark, and in the cradle lay a wizened little creature. The pixies had taken their revenge.

Another favourite trick of the pixies is their magic eye ointment, of which there are several versions of one particularly infamous incident. A well-known midwife called Morada, a foreigner, lived near Tavistock. One night when a thunderstorm was raging she was woken by a loud banging on the door. When she opened it she found a 'squint eyed, little, ugly old fellow' who said his wife needed her help in childbirth. Before she could protest he had blindfolded her and lifted her on the back of his huge coal black horse with eyes like balls of fire and whisked her over the moor.

They arrived at a broken-down cottage where the woman lay on a filthy bed; two children crouched by the hearth. She seemed a middle aged, ordinary countrywoman. After the birth she gave the midwife some ointment and instructed her to rub it on the child's eyes. She did so and turning her back, rubbed a little on her own right eye. Suddenly the house had become a mansion, the children dressed in silks and satins and the woman lay on spotless linen covered by a rich fur rug. She and the children had become mortals. The midwife said nothing to the pixies about her use of the ointment and once more she was taken home on horseback.

A few days later she was in Moretonhampstead market and saw the pixie again; he was going from stall to stall stealing goods. She went up to him and asked how his wife and baby were doing. 'Can you see me?' he exclaimed sharply.

'To be sure, plain as the sun in the sky,' she replied. 'And I can see what you are busy at.'

'With which eye do you see this?' he asked. Foolishly she replied, 'The right'. Immediately he struck her on the eye making her partially blind for the rest of her life. She could no longer see the pixie.

Pixies could also be helpful sometimes, in the old days, helping to thresh corn, sweeping the kitchen and so on in return for a bowl of cream. In the 1930s, haymakers in Devon slopped cider on the ground or threw a few crumbs to the little people and I know one or two people in the South Hams who still leave a few apples on the ground for 'invisible friends'; this is known as pixie worting.

So what about being pixie-led or pixilated? The *OED* defines pixilated thus, 'bewildered, crazy, drunk, or a variation of pixie-led – in a daze'.

'Being pixie-led is the commonest reported experience of pixies,' writes Crossing. 'If you have been caught unaware by mist which makes every familiar object distorted so you lose all sense of direction and wander round in circles "proper mazed" it is probably the cunning little creatures who are trying to confuse you, leading you into boggy places for the fun of it. The recommendation to break the spell is well known if you encounter the little people – remove your coat or jacket, put it back on inside out.' He adds, 'if 'tis raining heavy it would be advisable to lose no time over this or be dapper, as we say on the moor or you will be soaked through'.

It is indeed sound advice, which I heeded myself after a talk I gave to the WI in North Bovey, some years ago. One of the members asked, 'Why do you always write about murder and mayhem, how about something suitable for the children, gentle and fairylike, perhaps pixies?'

I replied, 'Unwilling as I am to disillusion anyone, I would like to assure you that some pixies are far from gentle, they can be both vindictive and sadistic, perhaps not so different from some human beings. I would add that they are not some airy fairy imaginary beings who only existed many years ago, they are certainly alive and well today as many people to whom I have talked have seen them and been pixie-led which can be quite terrifying.' There was general laughter. But I should have known better than to tempt fate.

After the meeting one of the members asked if I would like to go back to her house for a drink and to discuss the subject further as it fascinated her and she thought the whole thing rather far fetched. I said it was virtually on my way and I should be delighted. We chatted as we drove, when suddenly I realised I hadn't the slightest idea where I was, even though I knew the area pretty well. There was not one familiar piece of road or landscape, it was totally unrecognisable, I could have been on the moon.

'I'm so sorry, I think I must have taken the wrong turning when I left the village,' I explained. 'Not to worry, round the next corner is the road I am looking for.' I added 'I think' under my breath. My companion said, 'We're nowhere near my house, we should have reached it by now'.

We drove on slowly, a slight chill of fear surrounding us. There was no corner, no familiar road, I was completely disorientated and naturally there was no signpost in sight.

Suddenly I remembered those fatal statements I had made about the mischievous pixies, something I did not usually do in public. So I was being punished. I was being pixie-led.

I stopped the car, threw open the car door, dragged off my jacket and turned it inside out. My startled companion was sure I had lost my senses. 'Please don't worry,' I said as I got back in the car, 'at least you know I was not making anything up.' As I closed the car door, the road at once became familiar and we continued our rather silent journey; in fact so silent it was easy to hear the chuckling laughter that had filled my ears as I turned my jacket.

I was in good company, however, for this sense of losing direction and wandering in helpless circles has happened to scores of perfectly ordinary people. In Tudor times Sir John Fitz (he was the grandfather of Lady Mary Howard and a friend of Sir Francis Drake) and his wife, who owned large estates round Tavistock and Okehampton, were riding on the moor near Princetown when they found themselves hopelessly lost on ground with which they thought they were familiar. They realised they were being pixie-led and began to feel exhausted and thirsty as it was a hot summer's day. Suddenly, they came upon a spring of pure water, which they certainly did not remember existed in the area; turning their coats inside out they then recognised their surroundings, and were able to find their way home after slaking their thirst in the welcome water. In gratitude Sir John placed a stone above the spring bearing the initial JF 1568, now known as Fitz's Well.

This brings me to my final pixie story and perhaps the least written up, but most famous, of Jan Coo who was, without doubt, pixie-led to his death.

The story begins at Rowbrook Farm, which stands on the slopes below Sharp Tor, on the track that leads down from the B3357 at Bel Tor near the farm gate. A branch of the French family occupied this farm when the Stuarts ruled. Sitting by the log fire in the kitchen, sipping cider, Algy May, a tenant sheep farmer, told me about Jan Coo who, in the mid 1800s, was pixie-led from this very kitchen.

In the past, all farms employed young apprentices who often lived with the family for 20 years or more, a tradition that continued until after the Second World War. The apprentice would receive no pay to begin with but the farmer would feed and clothe him, and teach him all he knew about cattle, horses, reaping, shearing, planting and thatching. Usually he was given the coldest place in the kitchen by the door, this was 'his place', but if he was obedient, quick and went to church on Sunday, he grew up like one of the family, he was never unemployed and usually had a cottage on the farm for life.

Rowbrook Farm where Jan Coo was pixie-led (© Nick Wotton)

This should have worked for Jan Coo, but it was said he was 'coveted by the River Dart' which 'takes at least one heart a year', probably for the pixies.

One winter evening Jan burst into the kitchen where everyone was preparing to sit down to the evening meal. He shouted to them to 'come outside, quick!' The sound they heard made the hairs stand up on the backs of their necks. A wailing voice like a banshee was calling 'Jan Coo ... Jan Cooooo'.

Quickly, they lit their lanterns and ran down to the riverbank from where the sound came. But now the cry had stopped and there was no sign of a living soul. They were glad to return to the warmth of the kitchen, but no sooner had they closed the door than the cry came again, more insistent than ever. A couple of them and Jan ran down the rutted track but still they found no one. The next evening exactly the same thing occurred, but this time one of them said, 'Tis they pigsies, I reckon'. They were all more than satisfied with this explanation of pixies, so when it came plaintively again, they ignored it.

Twelve months passed. In the spring, when they were at work one evening, they heard it again, 'Jan Cooooo', more insistent than ever. This time they could tell it came from Lang-a-Marsh Pit, which was well known to be a place where pixies gathered. Jan went down alone, but out of sight behind him one of the others followed.

Reaching Look-a-Tor Jan started to leap from boulder to boulder across the swiftly flowing river. He was making for the Pit. The man behind kept shouting his name as he stood on the bank, for he did not fancy risking his own life. Still Jan took no notice. As the man watched, suddenly Jan was not there, it was simply as if he had vanished into thin air, never existed.

It was late evening now and dark. There was nothing the others could do until morning, when the valley filled with the sound of human voices calling for Jan Coo. All that happened was that the valley echoed the name back in return. Alive or dead Jan was never seen again and none would argue but that the little people had taken him to their own world beneath the marsh.

So go pixie hunting by all means but be sure to wear some kind of coat and turn it 'foreback behind' ...

4

Phantom Houses – Now You See Them, Now You Don't

C an time stand still? Is there a subtle link between this world and the next, making this happen? I have come across many stories from people who feel they have stepped into a parallel world, unknowingly seeing things as they once were, then returning to the same spot to find that the beautiful house they saw only yesterday is actually a ruin. Others experience the past through inherited memory; a place or scene seems familiar to them, even though they know they have never visited it before, and then they later discover that it has some significance in their family's past.

The parallel world theory is a quite common belief among many people who maintain that buildings which have been inhabited can leave some kind of impression if they are destroyed, then weather or atmospheric conditions can reproduce an image and trigger off a supernatural phenomenon. It is an experience often shared by more than one person and is one of the most realistic manifestations of ghosts from our past.

To illustrate this I will begin with the quite extraordinary experience of a friend, Mary, who was walking round the lovely Devon lanes behind our house in the Ogwell area near Newton

Abbot, one hot August afternoon, when she stopped for a moment for a breather. Leaning on a farm gate, she saw a small cottage, which was like the picture on a chocolate box, in fact it was almost too traditional to be true. It had a thatched roof, a rose rambled over the cob walls and old-fashioned lilies edged the brick path. She was furious with herself for not having her camera with her.

She described the cottage in detail when she got home and persuaded her husband Charles, a rather unwilling walker, to visit it with her the next day. She had carefully marked the position of the building on a map, noting various trees and part of an old privet hedge that edged the garden.

When they reached the spot, she could not believe her eyes. There was nothing, no cottage, no garden path, just grass and a few rocks and stones. The gate had gone but two rotting posts stood where once it had hung. On a slight mound behind the hedge was a pile of stones, which had formed a wall of cob.

The whole atmosphere was also different, the sky had clouded over and a chill breeze blew up whirls of dust from the stones. Charles said obviously she had been mistaken but poor Mary was in tears; she knew for certain she had seen the cottage on exactly the spot where they stood.

Later over tea I reassured her. 'Don't worry, you aren't mistaken.' I glanced at Charles who was still waiting to be convinced. 'A cottage did once stand there, it was empty for many years and gradually fell into decay until eventually the farmer who owned the land had it demolished. I went to the library in Exeter and found a very old map of the area, and comparing it with my map I saw a cottage called "Heartsease" had once stood there.'

I don't know whether Mary was more excited at having seen such a sight as a phantom cottage or the fact that her husband, rather sheepishly, had to apologise, although he could hardly be blamed for his conclusion.

Talking to Theo Brown, she told me of a book by Elliott O'Donnell, *Haunted Britain*, in which he wrote of a cottage near Chagford. Two ladies, who were on holiday in the district, came upon it during their rambles and thought how pleasant it would be to stay there. A notice on the door stated 'Bed and Breakfast'.

A young girl answered their knock and they asked about the notice and if any rooms were vacant. 'Yes m'dear, we takes in visitors but we be full booked this year,' she replied. The ladies explained that they were enquiring about the following year and the girl was happy to accommodate them saying, 'I looks forward to seeing you then'.

Later in the week the visitors could not resist returning to have another look at the cottage, which they described as 'out of their dreams'. They took the camera so they could show a photo to their friends. At first they thought they had picked the wrong spot, but after a few minutes there was no question about it, where a cottage had once stood there was nothing but a few bricks and pieces of rotten wood.

Back at the inn they were told by the innkeeper, 'I am not surprised ladies. Once there was a cottage, in fact several, where you described but they were demolished many years ago and only manifest themselves every ten or twelve years. Many people have seen them but always under the same weather conditions.'

Seeing them is one thing, but to actually speak to someone there would leave shivers down my spine for many years to come.

Mr J. L. Page in his book, *The Rivers of Devon*, 1893, tells the story of three young girls who were walking home from a late night party and took the wrong turning. Finding themselves lost near Buckfastleigh one of them noticed a cottage and suggested they ask for directions.

It was dimpsy, twilight, and they could see a lantern had been lit in the cottage window. As they glanced through they saw an old man and a young girl sitting by a log fire but even as they looked, the cottage simply vanished; they were left standing at the gate in the dusk.

Terrified they ran back the way they had come and eventually made their way home, exhausted.

The next morning they found their way back to the same place but all they could see was some stones marking where the foundations had been. This phenomenon was well known as 'The Phantom Cottage of the Moor'. When it had been a solid building it had a bad reputation for what took place there and by popular demand had been demolished.

There was another odd happening at Stoke Fleming when two ladies saw 'The Phantom of Harleston Manor' in 1939. They wrote to Theo telling her how they had once lived at Start House, parts of which were hundreds of years old. It stood at the end of a lane in the heart of the South Hams area, once a packhorse track.

One bleak November afternoon, the sisters, whose husbands were away fighting in the war, stopped for a moment during a walk and leant on a farm gate. Suddenly, one of them said, 'I thought you told me there was no house here?' Looking across the valley, standing in the trees, they saw a great manor house and, as they watched, more buildings appeared beside the house.

They knew at once it could not be real because they were well acquainted with the area from their constant walks. As one of them pointed out, 'It simply didn't LOOK real. It was perfect but with no solidarity, no substance; as we stared, after five minutes or so it gradually faded away.'

The following spring one of the sisters, whose husband was home on leave, walked down to the site with him. When she pointed to the spot where the house had stood he said, 'It is a wonderful site for a house, it is obvious some building once stood here as the grass which grew on the level area where the foundations would have been is quite different from field grass'.

As a final note to the sisters' extraordinary experience, several people living in Start House earlier had heard horses galloping in the lane but never actually saw them. There seems to be no doubt they came from the stables by the 'ghost' house.

Of the many letters I have received on this subject, one came from Derrick Warren whose job in 1955 was to revise the 1:2500 Ordnance Survey map in the Haytor area. He was on the hill below the village looking down towards Bovey Tracey, checking the old map to see what new buildings needed to be recorded and other changes such as hedges, which had either been removed or replaced. He also had to record any new house names.

About a mile away, in a rather remote wooded area, he could see a small cottage, which did not appear on his map. Clothes hung on a line and smoke came from the chimney so it was obvious someone lived there. The next day when he explored the area he could find no trace of a building. He must have made a mistake and being busy, and anxious to get on with the job, he decided to leave it.

Two weeks later, when he was working in Brimley, the lady whose house he was surveying invited him in for a coffee. 'She asked me if I had an old map of the area as she was trying to identify a cottage she had seen, but could not find on her map. She had walked over the hill, stood looking back at Brimley and Bovey, and could see a cottage, near the lane, which appeared to be occupied. She had actually found the lane but no building of any sort in the area. She tried in vain to find out more about it from everyone including the District Council, but there was no record at all.'

Derrick told her of his own sighting which tallied exactly. He went back and scoured the whole area but also drew a blank. The only clue was that roughly where he thought the cottage must have stood was a hedge made of myrtle. This was much favoured for use as a hedge in the old days for gardens as it is evergreen, and also cattle and sheep will not eat it because it is bitter.

In 1956 Derrick was living in Somerset and saw a book by Ruth St Leger Gordon, *Folklore and Magic of Dartmoor*. In it she had written about the sighting, by three people, of a cottage which did not exist. It was on the southern slopes of Dartmoor. He called on Mrs St Leger Gordon at Sticklepath and told her his story. Before he had finished she asked him not to reveal the actual location. She then called her neighbour in to act as independent witness. They marked separate maps with their respective locations and gave them to him. The neighbour confirmed they were identical. No one has yet been able to solve this extraordinary story.

Another letter I received came from Joan Amos of Peter Tavy. Her story is an amazing example of inherited memory. Joan said she had a psychic gift, experiencing flash visions or prerecognition dreams, which she did not understand until something else happened at a later date which triggered a connection.

Joan's father died when she was quite young, leaving her mother to bring up three children. So at the age of four, as she was the eldest, Joan was sent to live with her grandparents.

Some years later, when she herself was married with children of her own, Joan was invited to a fancy dress party near Plymouth with a friend. The venue turned out to be a big house approached by a long drive. Joan said, 'I began to get an eerie feeling. Although the sun was shining through the leaves of the trees, I felt freezing cold and was trembling all over. Where the trees ended stood a large manor house where workmen were painting the woodwork. They told us we had got the date wrong, the party was next week, but there was a sports day and fete at the nearby village. As it was a few miles away, I went to the front door to ask if there was a bus service. An elderly gentleman answered and invited me into the parlour; he said he would phone to find out the bus times.

'The room was full of antique furniture, but what attracted my attention most was the view from the French windows which overlooked a green lawn with a sundial in the middle. As I stood looking out, I suddenly felt deathly cold as if I were going to faint. Everything became cloudy and the present seemed to fade away. It was as if I was in a different age. I had the most eerie feeling because I knew the view well, I recognised it. I had to have been in that room before, standing in exactly the same place, and yet how could this be possible. I had never even been in this area before.'

Apparently when the man came back he saw she looked quite ill. She told him she did feel a little faint and he fetched her a glass of water. Eventually she felt able to rejoin her friend, but all day she could not shake off the feeling that somehow, sometime she had belonged in that house.

Over the next 25 years she experienced the whole thing again many times, before finally she discovered the answer.

She was having tea with an elderly aunt when the conversation turned to family history. 'I asked her a question I had always wanted to resolve since my grandparents had died. How did grandma and grandpa meet? As is often the case I had never been much interested in that kind of thing when I was young and they were alive.

'Transport was difficult in my grandparents day, people didn't travel far but I did know that my grandmother was known as the

Belle of Trusham, where she came from, and it seems grandpa came from Lamerton near Tavistock.'

Her aunt told her that, as a young woman, her grandmother had gone into service as a nanny with the Rolls family. Her charge was young Charles Rolls, who later started the firm that made the Rolls Royce engine. This was in Wales and although the family were kind, she wasn't very happy so she responded to an advertisement in the paper for a parlour maid back in her native Devon and got the job.

In the meantime, the young man who was to become Joan's grandfather had a job as a groom in the same Devon house, having served apprenticeship as a stable boy. One of his jobs was to pick up visitors at the local railway station and among his passengers, on one occasion, was the pretty new parlour maid.

The rest was history. They fell in love, married, and the family gave them a big reception at the manor which Joan's aunt now started to describe in detail, she could even show her an old faded picture of the house. It was at this moment that Joan jumped to her feet shouting, 'Stop! Stop! Don't tell me any more, I know – it was Delamore House!' Her startled aunt wondered how on earth she knew that.

Joan explained her experience of 25 years before. She knew now why she had felt as she did when she walked into that parlour which her grandmother had looked after with loving care, probably standing exactly where Joan had, looking through the window at the garden until the view was imprinted on her mind and eventually on her granddaughter's.

So did Joan go back in time? Certainly, something strange happened to her on that day because she had known absolutely nothing about the story of her grandmother and grandfather or ever been in that house before in her life. Perhaps an explanation is unnecessary except that it proves there is a subtle link from the past to the present, which is beyond our comprehension.

5

Close Encounters over Devon

Devon seems to be a popular target for UFOs. Like crop circles, however, opinion remains divided as to whether or not the alien objects are genuine. Whatever your belief, the fact remains that many sightings of unidentified flying objects remain unexplained, such as the stories recorded here, which pose more questions than answers.

About 50 years ago a Mr A. W. Bearne of Southfield Avenue, Paignton, had his own close encounter with a UFO, which inspired him to write a book, *Flying Saucers Over the West*, dated 1968. His son D. P. Bearne kindly gave me permission to tell his story and quote from his book.

On Monday 30th October 1950, when Mr Bearne saw the flying saucer his first reaction was to report it to the police and the local paper in Paignton. The reaction and reports he received from Air Force personnel lead him to observe, 'I cannot think any intelligent person after reading these reports can fail to realise that flying saucers do exist and are not fictitious.'

At 10 pm that October evening, Mr Bearne was walking to his home in Southfield Avenue when he saw a light over his head and a funnel-shaped stream of white flames descending, pointed end first, in complete silence. He described them as 'fingering' downwards and half a minute later they disappeared from sight beyond the roof of the house. The apparition came to view again in a ball of fire, moving horizontally now over Paignton towards Churston Ferrers and Higher Brixham at about 500ft. Suddenly, it again altered course with a huge disc in front, from which the flames receded as it climbed upwards.

The next day, the local paper, the *Herald Express*, carried the following report in the late news column: 'Flying saucer seen over Paignton; the first report of one over the West Country came from Mr Bearne of Southfield Avenue, Paignton.'

The following day, 1st November, reports came in from other eyewitnesses, too many to quote here in full, who also stressed there had been no sound but a stream of fire. Mr Bray, a fisherman, saw it from the bunk of his boat in Torquay outer harbour. Mr Cove Clarke of 9 Marine Drive, Paignton rang Mr Bearne to tell him he had seen a similar occurrence in 1945 when he was on duty as a special constable. The crew of a liberty boat from HMS *Defiance* in Devonport Dockyard saw it. On Sunday 5th November, the *Sunday Dispatch* printed an account of the sighting and said independent witnesses at places as far apart as Woolacombe, Exeter, Cullompton and Sidmouth had seen it. In the *Herald Express*, on the 13th and 28th December, there were details of two more sightings by two cowmen in Kingswear and three men in Penzance. In the same paper, four years later, on 2nd of November 1954, two Torquay men were reported to have seen about 15 mysterious balls of fire in the sky. On the previous day, at 3.45 pm Mr Branson, of 50 Bampfylde Road in Babbacombe, had seen a cluster of fireballs over Weymouth.

More and more witnesses came forward to confirm these reports including Mr Hines of Stover Golf Club in Newton Abbot, who had been on the front at Exmouth when he had seen the same objects. In all these reports nobody has been able to refute the suggestion that these were interplanetary visitors.

There is a theory that some more recent 'booms' and 'bangs' in the Devon sky have been caused by Concorde. Mr Robert Wyse, press officer at the Torbay UFO Centre, has pointed out that, as these were often heard at night, they could not be attributed to Concorde. They could, however, be caused by unidentified flying objects travelling at supersonic speed. In fact the centre's records show that noises had been recorded when it was known that both Concordes were grounded.

Mr Wyse has kindly given me details of literally dozens of sightings and occurrences connected with UFOs all over Devon, some of which I give here.

On 14th April 1978, Mrs June Amons of Tavistock saw a saucer shaped craft hovering over the town for three minutes in a halo of light. It was also spotted by a lady in Plymouth at the same time. In March the same year, Stephen Wright and Paul Groves, from the UFO centre in Torquay, were on sky watch at Watcombe and saw orange lights moving over Teignmouth. On 2nd April, several members of the centre saw an object moving from Stoke-in-Teignhead towards Babbacombe and out to sea, it was a large circular object with three white lights rotating in the centre. On 10th May, Mr and Mrs McClusky were awoken in their home at Haytor by a loud rumbling noise at 8 am. Two orange objects were stationary on the hill at the back of their house, one moved off at great speed with the noise of a rocket, followed by the other. Soon after, two RAF jet planes appeared and followed the course of the UFOs, as if chasing them. The list is endless, made all the more intriguing by the lack of any rational explanation.

In April 1981, the *Western Morning News* carried a story in which UFO investigators said they had evidence that a holidaymaker had been taken aboard an aircraft from a field on the outskirts of Budleigh Salterton. The man involved was a 35-year-old bachelor from Kingston on Thames who was on a cycling tour.

On the night of the 21st April, he was camping in a field when, at 4.30 am, he saw two bright lights near a farm building and decided to see what was happening. He walked along the road from the field where he was camping and halfway along he saw another brightly lit object on the other side of a small stream. At that moment it was as if someone had hit him from behind with a blunt instrument, throwing him to the ground.

In front of him was an oval shaped object with exterior lights flashing. He had a sharp pain in his head and back and, struggling to his feet, he felt freezing cold, although the evening was mild.

He had no idea how long he had lain on the ground but as he got up, the object increased in brightness and flew off to join two more in the sky. Walking along the road, back to his tent, one of them started to follow him, swinging backwards and forwards liked a pendulum. It eventually flew off as he reached his tent.

With trembling hands he packed his case, and hurriedly left the area. The time was now 6.35 am, which meant he had been away from his tent for two hours but it only seemed a few minutes. Reaching Exmouth he stopped for a rest, as he was totally exhausted and, taking off his shoes and socks, he found his left ankle was very swollen with two small puncture marks in it.

As he cycled home, and for the next few days, he was convinced he was being watched. His case was investigated by experts, who concluded he had been taken aboard some kind of craft after he was stunned, and medically examined.

This incident reminded many people of the case of Genette Tate, who disappeared in 1978, at the age of 13. Her body was never found although her bike lay in the lane where she had disappeared, the wheels still revolving, seen by her two companions who came round the corner within seconds. There had been no sign of a car. This was near Aylesbeare where recently there had been two independent sightings of UFOs and scorch marks in a nearby field. Aylsbeare is on the ley line which passes through Throwleigh church, Drewsteignton church and on to Aylesbeare, so maybe there is some supernatural force at work here.

In 1993 I read a brilliant interview, by Jack Holman, with Doug Cooper who lived and worked at Honiton as an investigator for the British UFO Research Association. He has much information not commonly known and was kind enough to talk to me about this. His view is that, 'When you sift through the evidence and discard the practical jokes I reckon you are left with one in ten genuine reports. Space engineers and scientists at NASA are convinced of their existence, which is too overwhelming to be ignored. More and more people are querying whether man on earth is the only intelligence around. I think it is inconceivable that he is.'

Nobody can prove him right or wrong and Doug goes on to say, 'I am not trying to convince anyone, keep an open mind, open, not blank. Don't knock what you can't prove wrong.'

Nick Pope, who ran the Ministry of Defence UFO desk Secretariat (Air Staff) 2a, is the British Government's expert on the UFO. He is a strong believer and has written a book on the subject, *Open Skies, Closed Minds*. No one can refute his claims for while he was at the Ministry, between 1991 and 1994, he collected a hard core of reports, defying any rational explanation. Earthly science is at a loss to explain the extraordinary speed of UFOs or 'Silent Vulcans', described as 'The Flying Triangles'.

Most credible of all is the report from two policemen, Clifford Waycott and Robert Wiley, who on 31st March 1993 were driving along the A3072 on patrol near Okehampton when they saw a bright light in the sky. As they neared Holsworthy this light was behaving as if it had been waiting for their reaction, sailing along a little way ahead of them above the treetops, so low and silent it could not have been an aircraft.

They radioed their HQ saying they were going to investigate. The faster they moved, however, so did the object, until they were doing 90 mph, round corners, climbing hills and sweeping down valleys, but they never got nearer to it than a few hundred yards. At last it was obvious they must slow down or have to report crashing a car while chasing a UFO, which would certainly make their superiors very suspicious.

They contacted the RAF station at Chivenor who stated they had no aircraft in the air, particularly any answering their description of hovering and then changing to such supersonic speed. Within a few hours an increased number of reliable witnesses had also seen these objects, including the BBC engineers manning the transmitter on Dartmoor, as well as more police, from Plymouth Docks and other places all over Devon. They all spotted the extraordinary craft between 1 am and 1.30 am, all independent of the others.

Later, Nick Pope spoke to the police and the BBC engineers, and from their detailed description confirmed it was certain the lights they had seen were not from normal aircraft, they were simply unidentifiable. He told me, 'By lunch time it was obvious I was right at the centre of the biggest wave of UFO sightings ever reported in Britain. No planes answering this description were airborne by the RAF anywhere in the area.' He added, 'In Britain over 400 sightings are reported each year, there are probably many more but people are afraid of being ridiculed'.

It does seem that a technology far in advance of our own penetrates our air space. Possibly the media is muzzled by the powers that be for fear of panic, so there is a cover up of the true facts. Whether we agree or not is our privilege, but one thing is certain, the UFO is not history; when seen they will continue to be chased by the RAF and American Air Force, recorded on radar, filmed and photographed.

So it seems there is something there in outer space and a great deal of it appears over Devon.

6

The Most Haunted Castle in England

The list of supernatural experiences people have had at Berry Pomeroy is phenomenal. I have to warn you, though, that many people to whom I have spoken admit that immediately they approach the Gatehouse they feel an unreasonable depression, fear, loneliness and desolation. Pam Brewer, who had taken her children there to play, said that, having got out of the car and crossed the yard in great excitement, they suddenly came rushing back saying they didn't like the place. The smallest girl, Angie, exclaimed, 'Something horrid touched my hair!'

The first time I visited it I certainly felt a deep sense of an eerie atmosphere. To begin with, the situation of the castle is fascinating. Perched above the Gatcombe valley, it combines fortified remains within a flamboyant mansion. It was the home of the Pomeroy family, the manor having been given to Ralf de la Pomerai of Normandy by William the Conqueror for his part in the Battle of Hastings.

In the mid 16th century, it was sold to Edward, the brother of Jane Seymour, but after 1688 no other member of the family lived there and by 1800 it was completely deserted. It is now maintained by English Heritage, who succeeded the Environment Ministry in 1977, but as it had been left alone for so long it is not strange that ghosts have taken over.

Many visitors to the castle have experienced the unsettled atmosphere, described by Pam Brewer and her children, and which I myself felt. Miss White of Torquay told me some friends of hers had walked up to the castle and passed some cottages that were derelict, with ruined barns. It was a scene of complete desolation with an extraordinary aura of evil. In fact, one member of the party was so upset she went back to the car. As the others walked on they saw scenes of utter ruin.

So fascinated were they that they had to return several days later. At first, they thought they had come to the wrong place, in fact, they simply could not believe their eyes. There had been a complete transformation, buildings were restored and re-roofed, and gardens well tended. The only explanation must be that on their first visit they had regressed in time, and then, on returning, saw it as it is today. There are other examples of this phenomenon in Chapter 4.

There is no record of anyone actually living in the Tudor part of the house, which Cromwell may have destroyed, although there is a theory that it was struck by lightning and burned down. This would fit in well with the long history of violence, murder and suicide in which the castle is steeped.

There is the story of two young Pomeroy knights who held the castle during the Rebellion in 1549, when the edict went out that all castles must be destroyed. Rather than submit to the degradation of seeing their home ransacked, they hid their gold and other valuables, then, blindfolding their horses, galloped them over the cliff into the valley below. Several people have testified to hearing the sound of horses' hooves late at night in the valley.

When the Ministry of Environment was doing work at the castle, I spoke to Jack Hazzard, foreman at the time, and he had had several cases of people feeling suddenly faint, or convinced that the buildings were a menace, intending to do them harm.

My cousin Joan, home on holiday from South Africa with her daughter, was walking along the ramparts and, as they approached St Margaret's Tower, Joan could go no further. She felt a horrible, cold, antagonistic aura enclosing her. Her daughter had gone on down towards the dungeon and she actually saw a white lady. In a panic, she rushed back to her mother.

Berry Pomeroy Castle

Sheila Ellis, who ran the tearoom at the castle, told me a clergyman and his wife had been on a visit and, as they went through the Gatehouse, his wife had suddenly fainted. When she came round she said she had seen a girl about the age of their daughter, dressed in blue, who beckoned to her. Her face seemed contorted with such an evil expression it had made her faint.

Sheila also showed me a clear photo she had taken of the front of the house and gazing out of one of the first floor windows is a man appearing to be from the Stuart period. So what are the foundations of these hauntings, which so many people have felt?

It seems two sisters, Eleanor and Margaret de Pomeroy, were in love with the same man. Eleanor, the elder, was the mistress of the castle, but was jealous of the younger and more beautiful sister so she shut her up in the dungeon, starving her to death. It is Margaret's ghost that is said to walk the ramparts dressed in long white flowing robes, beckoning to the beholder to come and join her in the dungeon below.

Another haunting was brought into prominence when a certain eminent doctor, Sir Walter Farquhar, wrote of it in his memoirs. He had been called to attend the wife of the steward of the castle. While he waited in the parlour, the door opened and a young lady, evidently in great distress, passed him and went up the small staircase, giving no reply to his enquiries as to whether he could be of any assistance. His patient was very ill, however, and for the moment he forgot the incident.

A few days later he recalled the apparition and asked the steward about the young lady. The man's face turned ashen as he said, 'Now I know my wife will die!' The doctor said this was nonsense because she had passed the crisis and was well on the road to recovery.

Doing all he could to reassure the man, the doctor went about his daily visits, forgetting the whole matter. Some days later when he returned to see his patient, she had died.

The steward had told the doctor that the apparition was a daughter of a former Baron of Berry Pomeroy, who had borne a child to her own father and was so horrified with guilt she had smothered it in the same room. The omen, her appearance just before someone's death, as the doctor himself had witnessed, never failed.

Hamlyn Parsons wrote in 1960 about an incident which occurred when he took his red cocker spaniel, Bruno, to the castle once for a walk. They walked round the walls and into the dungeons, but whenever he approached St Margaret's Tower, from whatever direction, the dog went into paroxysms of terror. 'Even when I carried him in my arms facing away from the Tower he went almost mad with fear.'

Finally, I have my own creepy experience of Berry Pomeroy castle. I had been out filming a documentary for the BBC, when I suggested to the cameraman that we visit the castle one evening, with a view to getting some 'ghostly' footage to flog to the television station.

It was a warm summer night with a sickle of moon and we went across the ramparts and down into the dungeon. The cameraman flashed his torch round the damp walls and tested his camera.

'Would you believe it, the damned thing has jammed, now that's something that has never happened before.' I had my tape recorder, however, with a fresh battery and very sophisticated new mike.

The place seemed to be getting noticeably colder, like something tangible. There were also some odd thumps and a sound of a door clanging, which was impossible as all the doors were off their hinges.

We were glad when the sun rose and we could go home to eggs, bacon and hot coffee. I switched on the tape recorder, which was standing on a small table by the stove. It simply leapt from the table, as if it had a life of its own. Jeff picked it up, shook it and switched it on again. We ran the whole tape and it was completely blank. Twenty-four hours later he had his film developed, he had taken several shots in and around the dungeon and, not much to our surprise, the film was also blank. Even the one he had taken of me to finish it was simply plain black.

I have never been back to Berry Pomeroy. Ley lines pass over there, which I believe very firmly to be both benign and evil, and I am not one to tempt providence. However, if you want to visit the most haunted castle in England it is open daily from March to October and lies off the A385, two and a half miles east of Totnes.

7

Mysterious Goings On

'It was while I was in the bathroom that it all began, I was washing my hands, when I felt what was obviously a finger being drawn down my neck. The finger was ice cold.'

Thus begins a spine chillingly true story, which I reproduce here with the kind permission of the *Western Morning News*. The writer wishes to remain anonymous and out of respect for the current owners of the cottage where all this occurred, so too must the location, other than to say these events took place in the oldest part of Chudleigh. The storyteller lived in the cottage between 1984 and 1985 with his, now ex-, wife, and there seems to be no reason for the troubles which both started and ceased with equal suddenness.

Returning to the ice-cold finger down our narrator's neck, naturally, when anyone feels such a sensation, the reaction is to swing round and see who is there. This he did but there was no other human being in the room with him and he could think of no explanation for such a feeling.

He went downstairs to the living room and found his partner, let's call her Mary, looking white as a sheet, cuddling their dog in her arms as if for security. As the man opened his mouth she interrupted, 'Don't say it because I already know. Something has just touched you hasn't it?' The man replied, 'Yes, but how do you know?' Her answer sent a chill through them both. 'Because it touched me too, something that felt like a finger.'

Some days later there was a further disturbance when they were in bed asleep, sometime after midnight. There was a pine dresser in the room that was fitted with Queen Anne drop handles on the drawers. One of these was rattling exactly as if someone was using a doorknocker, hitting it with something hard. They both woke with a start, assuming someone was at the door. When all went quiet they went back to sleep.

Later the same week, however, exactly the same thing occurred making it perfectly obvious the noise came from the dresser itself. The man said, 'I took it that one of the handles had been left stuck in the upright position, fallen down on the striker plate and bounced to a stop giving a knocking effect'.

He got up and checked all the handles which were all in the down position; when he tried to lift them none, due to age, would pass the level of half way position. He put as many of the six handles as he could into the raised position, then jumping up and down on the bedroom floor endeavoured to encourage the handles to drop and rattle. Not one did so, all staying in the midway position.

It was then they both came to the conclusion they were not alone in the cottage.

The next incident was when the storyteller thought he was alone in the front room reading the morning paper. In the kitchen was a wall-mounted glazed cabinet in which they kept the dinner plates, which began to rattle or vibrate against each other. He went to investigate. 'As I crossed the floor to the kitchen door the rattling ceased. I went back to my paper. No sooner had I sat down again than the rattling began once more. As I crossed the room the sound ceased. This happened four times. By the fourth I didn't bother to go and look again and the noise stopped.'

There were a couple more occasions, which caused more concern; the first was at night when they were in bed and our narrator awoke to find he was pinned to the bed. 'Whatever was holding me was not heavy, I don't believe it was touching me, but I was simply helpless as I lay there, totally unable to move my limbs or body. I shouted and Mary woke up and put the lamp on. At once the feeling was over.'

The final incident did not happen to either of the residents but to Mary's brother who came to stay overnight. He did not tell them what had happened until the next morning but he said:

'During the night I felt a jolt as if someone had bumped into the bed in the dark, then two hands seized me round the waist and started to try to pull me off the bed. They tried two or three times until I somehow grabbed my torch and switched it on, the light immediately stopped the effect.'

They made enquiries from all their neighbours if they knew of any previous problems but there had been no such happenings.

Eventually they went to their vicar but he could not help. The only conclusion they came to was that 'going public' with the story had stopped the incidents, which ceased without warning, just as they had started.

To me this seems very much like the usual behaviour of a poltergeist or 'noisy ghost', more of which in the next chapter. Frightening as the idea of such a spooky visitor in your home may be, there has never been a case of any actual physical harm, but they can none the less be terrifying, especially to anyone on his or her own.

8

Poltergeists – What Are They?

A good question, what are they indeed? Not knowing the answer myself, I searched for a definition on my computer. It seems that poltergeists are defined literally as 'noisy ghosts who hurl things around, drag people out of bed and also throw stones and set things on fire'. The first case I read about of such an unruly visitor was at Aller House, of which Theo Brown wrote in 1963.

Aller House stood just off the main road from Newton Abbot to Torquay, in the area of the present pub the Barn Owl that was once a farmhouse. It was a large, rather ordinary, Victorian-Georgian house later converted into flats.

I went to talk to a Mrs Mills who had lived nearby for 60 years. She remembered the house, which was solidly built with big rooms and a greenhouse, typical of the period, and that it had once belonged to the Powling family.

I wrote to Max Powling, but he was unable to help on the subject of poltergeists, stating, 'I lived there from the age of nine until I was 20, but sublimely unaware of anything other than a normal home between the years 1925 and 1937'.

He did tell me, however, that before they had taken over the house it had been offices for Devon Hide, Skin and Manure Company and it seemed their manager and bookkeeper Albert Victor Judd had committed suicide there because he had been involved in some financial fiddle or other.

During the war, the council took over the house and it was used for evacuees, before a Mr Weaver bought it. I went to talk to Mrs Weaver, and she told me, 'We lived there when we were first married. It was a big, inconvenient place with no hot water and it was us who turned it into flats. It was then the trouble started.'

She went on to explain, 'The hauntings were after my time. Eventually it was pulled down and all that is left is one wall with an old chimney and fireplace by the Barn Owl. The rest of the area was used for storage buildings for Unigate Foods.'

These troubles started in the flat occupied by a young couple called John and Carol Durston, who had moved there in August 1963. They both felt the presence of something abnormal, a menacing presence all the time; radios switched themselves on and off, doors opened and closed on their own, even furniture and crockery were broken. It got so bad they called for help from the local parson, the Reverend Gordon Langford, and he said he too could feel an evil atmosphere.

By now, Carol felt she simply could not be left alone in the place any longer. At the vicar's request, Bishop Dr Robert Mortimore held a 35-minute service, which included the sprinkling of holy water. Witnesses said they saw an apparition, which seemed to be someone in great distress.

On 8th December 1963, the *News of the World* reported more trouble when a Mr Leonard Culley who lived in the flat next door to the Durstons was working at his desk. He had felt as if someone had touched his back and experienced a sudden deathly coldness. Swinging round he saw a man of about 40 dressed in old fashioned business clothes glaring at him. As he jumped to his feet, the thing disappeared.

After the publication of my first book on mysteries, I received many letters from readers about their own experiences. One was from 'Penny of Paignton', who wished to remain anonymous. She had moved into a council flat and experienced an extraordinary coldness. At night it sounded as if someone were sorting through business papers, a soft rustling noise. Her daughter too was kept awake, but at first neither disclosed these facts to the other for fear of frightening them.

When they did at last speak of it, they decided it was probably noisy neighbours and tried all the normal methods of noise exclusion, including earplugs. Suddenly one night Penny saw a figure dressed in a black cloak over a white dress. Her little grandson, who happened to be staying with her, also saw 'this funny lady', but worse was to come because her daughter went through a complete change of personality, including dyeing her hair a ghastly shade of red, which was quite out of character.

Penny consulted a medium. She told her that probably in a former life some girl had been living there, most likely in the 1800s, who had evidently been unhappy and lonely, perhaps even raped and killed, and was now an earthbound spirit. The medium described her as young, about Penny's daughter's age, and with red hair. She thought it probable the visitations had occurred only to them because, previously, elderly and retired people had occupied the place. It was likely the girl was seeking someone her own age, Penny's daughter, and therefore manifested herself only during their occupation.

Mrs Nora Bertram wrote from South Zeal about a small terraced cottage, the middle one of three, in South Tawton. She said, 'The cottages had been built on a ruined site and I first noticed something odd when I was expecting my first baby. My husband was out at a bell ringing competition and I was watching television. Suddenly, there was an almighty crash as if someone had bumped into the sideboard, shaking all the china. I had the feeling that something or someone was in the room but I didn't feel frightened for some reason.

'As time went by, doors would open and bang shut on their own. Things put down in one place would appear in another and we would hear knocks on the front door, but when I went to open it and looked through the glass panel there was no one there. We began to call our "visitor" George.'

This went on for some years. The Bertrams had a daughter, Marcia, and one day Nora was washing Marcia's face in the bathroom, preparing to go out, when suddenly she felt a resounding smack on her bottom.

'It really hurt! I swung round expecting to see my husband grinning at me but he was downstairs at the other end of the house, he could not possibly have touched me. Marcia had neither seen nor heard anything and could not understand why I had shouted "Ow!"'

As Marcia grew older the family wanted more room and moved house, but just before they left they saw another side to George. It was exactly as if he resented them leaving; saucepans jumped from the cooker and the saltcellar fell to the floor and broke while Nora was cooking.

Nora threatened George with the vicar and exorcism and for a while all went quiet. Then one morning she opened the door of the china cupboard and a couple of mugs came clean off their hooks, smashing to bits on the floor. She said, 'I always thought it had something to do with Marcia because most things happened when she was around. She seemed to have a certain rapport with George, perhaps it was the spirit of someone who had been as happy in the cottage as we were and I feel quite privileged to have had such an experience in my life.'

Ann Brightmore-Armour, from Dawlish, sent me two strange little stories, which give authenticity to the existence of these spirits, or poltergeists, from the past. At one time she had worked in the food bar at the Mount Pleasant Inn at Dawlish Warren and here was a mischievous 'something' flinging jars of pickles and salad cream around.

She had also worked at Sefton Hall Convalescent Home in Dawlish. This was made from two 19th century houses and here too she had felt a malevolent presence. Not far from there is the Shaftesbury Theatre, well known to be haunted by 'Esmeralda', who turns the lights on and off. Very often, the cast arrive in the evening only to find every light in the building turned on, although they were certain they had been switched off before they went home the previous night.

So what conclusion can we draw from all this? One very decided view is that poltergeists are restless souls who have died in troubled circumstances. They pester the current inhabitants of their former dwellings because they want someone to release them from their predicament. Others believe it is the building, and not the ghosts of the past, which carries the aura of a troubled history and that is why these mysterious happenings occur. Either way, in general, the experiences of most people seem harmless enough, although it would not do to go meddling as you never know where evil might lie.

9

Ley Lines and Crop Circles – Fact or Fiction?

These were usually the two most popular subjects when I gave talks on the unexplained and supernatural in Devon and I would always refer people to Alfred Watkins' book *The Old Straight Track* for the basic information on ley lines. If you take the time, however, you can find your own ley lines, in which Devon is rich.

So what exactly are ley lines and how do you find them?

Put simply, ley lines are a pattern of alignments, which stretch across the landscape. A quick glance at a map reveals many features, apart from places, including roads, railways, rivers, contour lines showing height of hills, woodland etc. Maps are a record of history showing us places that were important in the past such as castles, hill forts, Roman villas, burial mounds, stone rows, circles, crosses and ancient trackways, holy wells, even moated manor houses, all of which provide clues pointing to the existence of that strange enigma, the ley system.

Alfred Watkins first coined the term in 1921, when he was looking for interesting features around his home area of Blackwardine in Herefordshire. The revelation came to him in a blinding flash when, out riding one day, he pulled up his horse at the top of a hill and gazed over the landscape below. He spotted a straight alignment passing through various ancient sites and churches and at that moment he became aware of a network of these lines standing out like glowing wires all over the surface of the country and intersecting at various sites, like an extremely intricate matrix.

Although Watkins' discovery caused some controversy, and still does to this day, no one had reason to think these were the ramblings of a mad man. Alfred Watkins was a very respected local merchant, an amateur archaeologist, inventor and naturalist, well known in academic circles. Following his key publication, *The Old Straight Track*, a Straight Track Postal Portfolio club was formed which enabled people to exchange and circulate information about, and photographs of, key ley lines. With the advent of the Second World War the club ceased to be but the interest in ley lines has been kept alive.

The principles behind the system still remain a mystery, although Watkins believed they could not have been a result of chance and was convinced that they had some origin in prehistoric routes, a theory which has been developed still further by people who believe them to be 'lines of power' with some kind of supernatural force. Many people have felt this force by touching standing stones, such as dolmans or menhirs, and experiencing a tingling sensation not unlike a mild electric shock. Of course Devon, and particularly Dartmoor, is rich in all these ancient stones and buildings.

The word 'ley' was chosen by Watkins because it is an old name for a clearing or enclosed field, many of which appear on the tracks from one landmark to the next. In fact, names are very important. Those most frequently found on ley lines are Burgh, Brent, Beacon or other forms of the word ley such as lea and leigh.

Ley lines are extremely easy to trace. One way is by dowsing, or water divining, for most of them run over underground streams, as I found in my own home, which had a watercourse running under it. I could trace 'my' ley line by standing in the churchyard at Highweek, near Newton Abbot, from where it ran to Haldon Belvedere to the north east, from there to Woodbury Salterton, onwards to Hembury Hill Fort. Turning round to the south west it ran to Berry Pomeroy Castle and on to Washbourne.

An even easier way of finding your own special ley line is by using a ruler and aligning it from a high point or prehistoric site on a map. Use the highest spots on hills, dead straight roads and river crossings and you will soon find a pattern emerging. Start by aligning three points in a straight line, then see if you can find a fourth and a fifth. If you manage five sites along about a 20-mile stretch, you have been successful in finding a ley line. They can vary in distance, from relatively short to a far-reaching line stretching way beyond that visible to the naked eye.

Alternatively, try dowsing or water divining. Don't be put off by the idea, it is an art almost anyone can learn, certainly sufficiently enough to find water, even if not its depth and flow. I use a bent clothes hanger! There used to be a college in North Devon which included dowsing on its curriculum, perhaps it still does, try the Internet.

If you want to follow the track of a ley line, one interesting five point alignment begins at Nine Maidens near Belstone and goes on to Hound Tor, passing White Moore Stone, Kes Tor and King's Barrow intersecting the south coast past Elburton's remains of a cross. There are also two very long leys, which cross at White Moor. The east to west ley connects Drewsteignton church, Spinsters' Rock, and Throwleigh church, westward to the line which touches the hut circles on Throwleigh Common, circles White Hill and on into antiquities over the Cornish border.

The enclosed map by David Whalley is self-explanatory and can be followed quite easily. Remember originally it was simply a trackway across country for man and horse with no more structure than that made by the user's feet, perhaps stoned or 'pitched' in soft places, but it is NOT a Roman road. As trading increased, people travelled further, so tracks crossed each other and trading posts were set up.

Picking up on Alfred Watkins' theory that ley lines were somehow connected to prehistoric routes, it is worth remembering that early man needed salt, flints and many other things, often not found in his own area, so he had to go further afield. One of these tracks, known as a 'salt way', often has names along its course such as White, Whit, Wicks, Weeks, Wishes or Wyches derived from the word for 'white', the colour of salt, which illustrate this need. There is a salt ley which comes through three crosses near Sticklepath, West Week, East Week, Way, Great Week, Bishop's Cross, Whitestone, and Bovey Tracey church to a spot on the shore of the Teign estuary (which my own ley crosses), an area well known for salt trading.

So get out your maps, pencils, paper and field glasses, plus your dowsing instrument and have a go at ley hunting. No one can object and it is fascinating. There is a British Society of Dowsers at Sycamore Barn, Hastingleigh, Ashford, Kent TN25 5HW. Tel: 01233 750253 or email bsd@dowsers.demon.co.uk.

Whilst ley lines certainly have mysterious origins, crop circles provide a constant source of debate between those who believe them to be a supernatural phenomenon and those who regard them as an elaborate hoax. I think the general consensus is that there are examples of both.

As harvest time draws near you can be sure reports of crop circles appearing in hapless farmers' fields up and down the country will become more frequent, although strangely enough not many incidents occur in Devon. I saw one good example just outside Newton Abbot in a field behind the Dartmoor Halfway pub. The field was steep and I should imagine not easy to work on, however it appeared overnight and stopped the traffic on the A381. One was also seen at Ware Barton near Kingsbridge and one outside Brixham on 14th July 1996, but for the past two or three years there do not seem to have been any being reported in this area.

Are crop circles created by shifts in the earth's magnetic field? According to Dr Colin Andrews, who has studied crop circles for 17 years, 20% are caused by eddies in the earth's magnetic field, the rest are man made; a point proved recently on Channel 4 by the man who runs a business doing just that!

So all but the simplest circles are hoaxes. If these, as Dr Andrews thinks, are formed by electro-magnetic eddies, this could account for the fact that some friends of mine at the BBC hit interference with their mikes when recording inside a circle.

Again, as with ley lines, Dr Andrews thinks the currents may work in tandem with underground water and mist in the air, and often along a layer of rock able to hold water known as an aquifer. These circles occur all over the world in grass as well as grain, many of course are never seen or reported.

Naturally with the modern day obsession with aliens, the circles have been attributed to little green men sending us messages or are said to be imprints of UFOs landing in the fields. Earliest reports go back to AD 815 in Lyon; actually both Stonehenge and Avebury could have been built on the sites of early crop circles.

In the early days witches and fairies were blamed, then along came the aliens. Now the electro-magnetic pollution caused by radio masts and mobile phones is the generally accepted cause. It is admitted that the earth does have energy lines of current which may intersect with the magnetic fields, bringing us back to where we started with ley lines. It is also possible that mini tornadoes could be responsible; although it is unlikely the patterns would be so intricate because whirlwinds usually travel in a circular motion.

Whatever your belief, farmers are as one in their view of the strange, detailed designs, they don't like them because flattened corn cannot be harvested. One farmer told me his field had been perfectly normal when he had gone to bed at midnight. At 4 am, when they started milking the cows, it had been flattened. There was no track beneath the patterns and the barley stems had been bent perfectly at the joint, something quite impossible to do by hand.

I asked Nick Pope, from the Ministry of Defence, for his opinion on crop circles, when I was interviewing him about UFOs. He said, 'My theory, at the end of the day, similar to UFO sightings, is that nine out of ten crop circles are probably a hoax, but there are always unknown phenomena, possibly with extra terrestrial connections'.

Ley lines you can prove exist for yourself but with crop circles, as the saying goes, you pay your money and take your choice. Fact or fiction, or a little of both, they still remain objects of mystery and fascination.

10

The Chapel on the Moor

Buried somewhere deep in the undergrowth at the foot of Haldon Hill, on Haldon Moor, are the crumbled remains of an old chapel with a grisly legend. It was built in the Middle Ages for the physical and spiritual welfare of travellers who were making the tiring journey to and from Exeter and was dedicated to St Mary.

The chapel was given into the care of a monk called Robert, whose duty it was to look after and hear confessions from the various travellers. But Lidwell, which was the name of the area, was a very lonely place, especially during the winter storms, and the isolation gradually began to tell on Robert's mind. He longed for comfort and companionship from his fellow man. Maybe, as is so often the case, the Devil found one more likely soul and just as in the story of Dr Jekyll and Mr Hyde a dual personality was formed.

By day he still seemed to be a dutiful and holy priest but at night Robert's nature changed completely. Putting on a dark cloak he would wander the moors until he found a lost and weary traveller. Pretending to be anxious for their welfare he would take the hapless victim back to the chapel. Here, using his knowledge of herbs, he would offer the visitor a warm drink heavily drugged, then he would plunge a dagger into the victim's heart, rob him of his wealth and throw him, whether he was now dead or alive, into a bottomless well, which stood just within the doors of the chapel.

Eventually Robert amassed an enormous hoard of jewellery and gold, so he built a safe hiding place in the altar of the chapel, which could be opened only by pressing a hidden spring. In time, when this cache was brimming over with goodies, he decided his next victim would be his last.

In this case it was a sailor homeward bound with much gold and silver, which he had earned through his long service in the navy. Like most sailors he was a naturally friendly chap so when warmed with drink and food, he entertained his host with tales from his many adventures at sea. The monk showed much interest; in fact his mouth literally watered when he saw what treasure the man was carrying.

At last he persuaded the sailor to kneel before the altar saying, 'I think it only fit my son you give thanks to the Lord for your safe return with such wealth. Let us pray together'.

As soon as the man knelt down and closed his eyes Robert, following his usual procedure, drew the dagger from his habit but unfortunately for him as the sailor raised his eyes to heaven he saw the shadow of the monk behind him with his dagger raised to strike. Leaping to his feet, the sailor raced to the door only to find it was locked.

By now Robert was beside himself with fury, never before had his dagger missed. He made ready to strike again but the sailor overpowered him and, kicking the dagger across the floor, he struck the priest with all his force. Screaming with terror, Robert missed his footing and fell, head first, into the well.

The sailor was horrified. He had no intention to do the monk any harm, only to protect himself. With his knife he managed to cut the lock from the door and ran out into the night to a nearby farm. The farmer was unwilling to believe his ears, he believed Robert to be a holy and dutiful monk, it was the stranger of whom he was suspicious. He was more than anxious to help Robert, however, and returned with the sailor to the chapel.

The two men lowered a bucket into the well but all they brought to the surface were the bones and rotting clothes of the monk's many victims. The farmer now believed the sailor's story and at that moment they heard moaning from the bottom of the well.

Pulling on the rope with all their force they hauled Robert, more dead than alive, to the surface. He crawled to the altar and pressed the spring, taking one last look at his treasure before he died from his wounds.

From then on no one dared go near the spot because an overpowering sense of evil hung in the air. The chapel and the well slowly fell into ruin but sometimes, at the dead of night, a violent struggle can be heard raging from the spot where once the chapel had stood and those who have the courage to keep their eyes open swear they have seen the bloated figure of Robert the monk twisting and writhing in an effort to pull himself out of the ooze that marks the site of the ruined chapel and the well.

11

Bowden – The Spookiest House in Devon

It has been said that you are never alone at Bowden House as there are so many ghosts there. So, if you happen to be visiting Totnes, be sure to take in this magnificent country house and see if you can spot some of its long-standing supernatural residents.

First, a bit of history about the house. The area was inhabited as far back as AD 800, when monks lived in the fortified homestead which stood on the site of the present Bowden House. Down the succeeding years, the house and surrounding buildings have had many owners. During the 13th century it remained a fortified house and then a priory and monastery. In the 15th and 16th centuries the Giles family rebuilt the old house into a vast Tudor mansion. By 1700, however, John Giles, who had been the richest merchant in Devon, became so poor he had to sell out to a wealthy farmer named Nicholas Trist. In 1976 the Petersen family bought it and in 1984 opened it to the public, complete with its hauntings.

I visited Belinda Petersen, the administrator, a few years ago and she took me for a short tour of the main buildings. She told me: 'For years we knew we had ghosts from the sightings that local people, builders and so on had experienced. I have to admit we played them down a bit as we thought it might downgrade an existing Grade 1 building. Anyway, so many visitors were commenting to the guides about the apparitions that a few years ago we thought we would include them in our history, having heard so many stories from both visitors and locals.'

She said she felt they were exploiting these spirits but her husband's view was somewhat different, 'They are simply justifying their existence by enhancing the house – keeping it alive if you can put it that way'.

Belinda explained: 'During the last 2,000 years generations have lived and died here so is not unexpected that many have made ghostly returns. After all, people say that stonework, even furniture may well hold memories, particularly in a house like Bowden which is built on ley lines. It has been a chosen site for both priories and monasteries so perhaps easier than usual for ghosts to find their way through. People are curious, ghosts are curious, they check on newcomers. It all started when the museum complex was under construction. The builders saw figures which now haunt the building inside and out.'

Belinda told me of two occasions on which she herself had actually seen ghosts. On a hot Tuesday in August 1980 she saw a man dressed in Tudor clothing on the lawn; she thought perhaps he had come from Totnes Elizabethan Day, held in the town each week. She went forward to greet him but he simply vanished as she watched. In no way could he have left without being seen.

On another occasion she saw a lady visitor in the Queen Anne Room who was holding a small branch of a beech tree saying it was to ward off evil spirits in the house. Belinda was able to assure her all the spirits are benign and friendly.

The largest numbers of sightings seem to occur during the busy part of the season, especially during August as it is said ghosts live off the warmth and electric energy generated by a crowd of people. There was one famous incident, however, on Christmas Eve in 1988, when a guest in the pink bedroom was woken by the sound of monks chanting. Someone stood by her bed holding her hand in a gentle grasp, telling her not to be frightened; this brought her comfort and a great feeling of well-being.

Nicholas Trist put in the main staircase in the early 1700s and it is here the most famous ghost is generally seen. Again it was August, Bank Holiday in 1988 to be precise, when two ladies coming down the stairs said they saw a figure coming up towards them, a little girl aged about eight in a long blue dress with a white lace collar. She had shoulder length hair tied back with a ribbon and a thin face with rather sunken blue eyes. She appeared as solid as a normal child, in fact they had to walk round her to avoid running into her, but when she reached the landing she simply disappeared. It seems that this could have been the ghost of Alice Eteson who died of tuberculosis at the end of August 1765, at the age of seven.

Alice Eteson lived with her parents in the small room at the top of the stairs (now the pink bedroom). Her father, Simon, was employed on house restoration and her mother was a seamstress.

The first time Alice was seen was by Stella Henderson when standing outside the south west facade of the house during the 1960s. She saw Alice looking out of the window of the pink room.

Incidentally, it is well known that animals sense ghosts when humans do not and Sukie, the resident Bowden cat, would not

Bowden House, Totnes

walk into a certain room in the normal way but jumped over the threshold to a height of about 3ft as if there was some obstruction in her path.

Another familiar ghost at Bowden is a lady in a white dress. She always appears on the back stairs dressed in finery with a fontanelle head dress. It was apparently quite a common practice in the 18th century for the master of the house to have one, or even two, 'live-in' mistresses and it is thought this was one of Nicholas Trist's mistresses who was jealous of his wife Elizabeth. She felt she should have been the legitimate mistress of the house, instead of being confined to the back quarters.

One visitor thought this lady could be the ghost of Alice Eteson's mother, Tessa, who never got over the death of her little girl and keeps returning in an effort to unite with her. She said, 'I do not understand how they can be in the same house and not united, the feeling of sadness will remain until they are'.

There are more experiences from visitors to Bowden, of which Belinda kept records. One concerns a building in the grounds that was rented by a honeymoon couple, Spike and Marion, who then decided to keep on the occupation for a year. After they had been there three months, Belinda met them one night about 10 o'clock, in the garden. Marion was very upset and told how an apparition had appeared in their bedroom at 4 am each morning for six weeks. At first it was very faint but every day it became more real and solid until in the last week it not only started talking to them but pushing them and shouting, 'Wake up, wake up!' Eventually, Mr Graham Wyley, a clairvoyant, exorcised a spirit, which was of Kenneth Durell who had died aged 53 on 8th October 1636. He was married but had an affair with a servant girl. When she became pregnant he could not face the shame and committed suicide. He had been employed at the house as a driver/coachman living above the coach house with his wife. He jumped from the top of the coach house, which in those days was one storey higher than it is now.

The irony was that the girl had lied, she was not pregnant but it was too late. Now Kenneth was haunting the stable area as an act of asking forgiveness for killing himself.

Two weeks after completing this investigation both the servant and the wife appeared as ghosts in the same area. Graham Wyley freed all the entities concerned who never returned to Bowden House.

As a rather intriguing footnote to this story, Spike and Marion moved to a house in Totnes and Kenneth's ghost moved in with them. They have become 'good friends' and he only appears to them in dreams.

Nicholas Trist's library retains its original Tudor oak panelling and over the marble fireplace is a carved oak chimneypiece dated 1585. Both visitors and guides have seen a man standing behind the door, a Georgian gentleman about 5ft 3ins in height, a full coloured solid ghost, if there can be such a thing, probably a manservant because he has a lot of silver braid on his frockcoat, resembling the uniform of a footman. On one occasion there were three or four ghosts in the room and the guide was in full flow when a woman started to brush at her skirt frantically saying, 'Get down, get down!' Everyone looked at her in astonishment when she said, 'I didn't think you allowed dogs in the house.'

'We do not madam,' the guide replied. To which her response was, 'Then who let this dog in?' There were no dogs in the household but the ghost of one had been scrabbling at her skirt and licking her legs. Phantom dogs do appear in this room but only to visitors.

Joan Petersen was taking round the 3 pm tour one afternoon when a Mrs Anne Leslie said, 'I love this house, I love this house', with a great deal of excitement and enthusiasm, although she had not actually been inside at the time.

When the tour was over she approached Joan saying, 'Now I will tell you what I saw in the garden before the tour. I was strolling near the Italian garden by the balustrade, when I observed an 18th century gentleman aged between 40 and 50, well rounded, standing with his hand on his hips, laughing heartily. He wore a tricorn hat, white shirt with very full sleeves and had buckles on his black shoes. He was a happy soul and his name was Wallace.' She was a clairvoyant, so was able to communicate with him, and she was to have many future experiences at Bowden.

Belinda on the stairs where the ghost of seven year old Alice often appears

Belinda's kitchen looks out on to an inner courtyard and a cottage called Singer. Early in the evening of the 23rd August 1993 she saw a new tenant, Jenny, looking very agitated and worried. Belinda opened her kitchen window and asked what was the matter. Jenny explained that when she went up the stairs in the cottage she heard someone's footsteps above her and the sound of a dress swishing on the carpet. The footsteps turned into the small bedroom on the right. Jenny said it had happened many times and had made her very nervous. There had also been many other happenings in the cottage.

Mr Rolle, a retired banker from New Zealand, rented Singer Cottage for several months while looking for a retirement home. During his stay, he clearly remembers waking up in the middle of the night to find a monk at the foot of his bed, at least 6ft 7ins tall wearing a brown habit. Where his face should have been was a bright blue iridescent light in the cowl. He remained motionless. Mr Rolle decided not to wake his wife for fear of frightening her. Instead, he watched the figure for some 15 minutes and deciding he meant no harm, turned over and slept. The odd thing is that when Mr Rolle was packing to move on, he found the notebooks in which he had written down all the occurrences in his daily life at Singer Cottage, but the pages where he had written this account were blank.

On 15th September 1994, two ladies in their early 30s spoke to Chris Petersen explaining that one of them was a complete sceptic and the other a true believer in the supernatural. They each gave their own account of the same incident. 'I stood in the Great Hall near the doorway, when I looked round I saw the dark shadow of a short woman in a long dress, she came towards me and went straight through me giving me an unbelievable sensation of blood rushing through my whole body and left me feeling frozen stiff.' The account was signed Rachel Hay, Bristol.

The second part of the story was by Melanie Baker. 'I was standing in the Great Hall near the doorway, my friend's shadow was cast on the chair near the door next to the fireplace, I was looking at the chair and Rachel's shadow moved, when I turned round she stood absolutely frozen. *She* hadn't moved but the shadow had. Looking at her face I knew something had happened.'

It seemed they had both seen the ghost of Nicholas's mistress, so who was the sceptic now?

One August afternoon in 1995, Mrs D. Watkinson saw a number of fully coloured ghosts on the front lawn. Three young ladies were playing croquet; one had fair hair parted in the centre and tied back in curls and ringlets, 20 to 30 on each side. She wore a long dress with plain low neckline and creamy lace edging. An older woman, also wearing a long dress, stood watching. This is the second occasion this group has been seen playing croquet. She also saw a slim young lady in a black dress she thought was a maid, carrying a tray.

In October 1997, there were a number of unexplained happenings and one lady said, 'I sat in the Tudor hall on the bench near the head of the table, when I had the physical sensation of being pushed down on to my seat. Each time I tried to resist and got up, I was pushed down again.'

This is similar to the experience of the man in the cottage in Chudleigh when he was pushed down and held in the bed. And also among the experiences of August 1998 is another very like that story of Chudleigh. Mrs J. Gale of Portsmouth wrote in the Visitors' Book, 'During my visit to the house I felt as if someone was gently blowing on the back of my neck. I turned around to see if anyone was close behind me but no. I checked to see if there was any door or window open causing a draught. They were all closed.'

There are literally hundreds of like sightings and experiences in this amazing house. During a charity evening Christopher Petersen was greeting visitors, one of whom, the Vicar of All Souls in Brixham, suddenly exclaimed, 'There are a lot of restless souls in this house!', a comment guaranteed to kill any conversation.

If you do see, or experience an encounter with, a ghost, you can either accept it at face value or come up with a logical explanation; perhaps it is a reflection or a trick of the light, or just plain wishful thinking. But when a house, such as Bowden, has such a colourful past, rich in history, it is not inconceivable that it is still home to some of the restless souls who lived there. Who can tell?

12

Big Cats and Other Ghostly Creatures

The mystery of the Big Cat has made news headlines, particularly during the 'silly season', for over 20 years. Today, every county up and down the country has its share of wild beasts roaming the countryside, usually cat-like and sufficiently large and sinister looking to be discounted as a domestic stray.

Actual photographic evidence of these beasts is thin on the ground, so the same images appear, encouraging people to join the search for the evasive creature prowling their neighbourhood. Devon has had its fair share of sightings from Devil's Cheesewring, Combe Martin and Haytor on Dartmoor, to Kingswood, Buckfastleigh and Ottery St Mary. Indeed, the British Big Cat Society was founded by Danny Bamping of Plymouth. The society now boasts 500 members and its headquarters, set up in 2001, are at Dartmoor Wildlife Park.

In 1977 a photograph was produced in Cornwall of an Abyssinian cat and Chris Mosier, author of *Mystery Cats of Devon and Cornwall*, remarked, 'Are the Big Cats as real as they seem?' This brought back an immediate response, via a letter to the paper, from Surgeon Vice Admiral Sir John Rawlin of Holne, who was in no doubt the answer was 'yes', having seen what could have been the Surrey Puma, on the A286 near Haslemere, himself.

Closer to home, there is the testimony from Josie Mackenzie of Modbury, South Devon, who was a definite sceptic until she saw a big cat for herself. She was walking her dog at Blackdown Rings when she describes seeing a mysterious black creature, which 'shot up' in front of her. She is now not so quick to doubt their existence.

Another incident at Shebbear, North Devon, has left the experts divided. A two-year-old Arab filly, called Jessica, had to undergo surgery after being discovered with a two inch deep wound either side of her neck, millimetres away from the jugular vein. Danny Bamping believes the wound could have been inflicted by a big cat, but Mike Thomas, from Newquay Zoo, is doubtful because he thinks the cat would have finished off his victim.

Whether big cats are real or not will remain as much a mystery as the existence of UFOs. Whilst big cats get a lot of media

Sightings of big cats regularly make headline news

coverage nationwide, other ghostly creatures, often far more sinister, get little coverage and yet have their place in the stories of the supernatural. For instance the White Bird of Oxenham is an unwelcome visitor to the Oxenham family. Seen by many members of the clan, the bird's appearance signifies imminent death.

Perhaps the most chilling of ghostly creatures spotted in Devon are the whisht hounds, spooky, black hounds, led by a Dark Huntsman who is either on foot or horseback. If you see these approaching, the advice is to lie flat on your face with arms and legs crossed and repeat the Lord's Prayer until all are passed.

The whisht hounds are thought to emerge from Wistman's Wood, on Dartmoor, every St John's Eve. In 1890 they were heard at Okehampton on Meldon Hill. At stables close by, horses being settled for the night became extremely agitated and sweaty and had to be rubbed down again.

The Whisht Huntsman, with his demon hounds, still lingers on Dartmoor, the Dewer Stone regarded as the spot he favours the most. A swarthy chap, he stalks his prey at night, when a storm is raging on the moor, but no one knows exactly what he hunts. It is said that all the animals' eyes glow like fire and are as big as saucers.

Theo Brown has compiled a list, running into hundreds, of reports of encounters with these sinister hounds, but is not sure if sometimes they may be the ghosts of dead pets, often said to represent people who died, or accompanying their dead owners. Some could be family dogs that come to warn of approaching loss. In most cases they are identified with a definite locality such as a house, a crossroads, a bridge or an old burial ground. Some patrol a section of road, often an ancient trackway or ley line.

Superstition is rife in Devon and many folk think these are ominous, signifying death within the year if you see them, some even say they are demonical and represent the Devil himself.

On the other hand, some ghostly pets protect their owners. There is a dog said to haunt a crossroads on the road down from Princetown to Roborough, where his master had been set upon and murdered. The phantom dog will attack any passer-by that he thinks may have perpetrated this crime.

There are also many stories about foxes and hares in ghostly form. It was commonly believed that witches could transform themselves into hares, more of which in a later chapter. In both Tavistock and Chagford similar stories are found of an old witch who possessed this gift of transmogrification. She would send her little grandson to the local Master of the Harriers to report the whereabouts of a hare. He would give the child two shillings and sixpence as a reward and he and his hounds would set out. The witch would show herself as a hare, leading the hounds for a good run. When she had had enough she would dart back into her cottage, changing back into human shape.

One night the hounds were too quick and nipped her leg as she scrambled back through her window. When the huntsmen arrived at the cottage they found her binding up her leg!

The Revd Hugh Breton, in his book *The Heart of Dartmoor*, tells of a man living near the Powder Mills at Cherrybrook who, after spending a pleasant evening at Postbridge one Christmas, got lost in the snow on the way home and his body was never found. One day, whilst gathering his flock of sheep, Master Smith of the Powder Mills Farm found the skull of a man lying inside a foxhole. More human bones were found nearby and it was decided these were the bones of the lost man. People still hesitate to pass the spot at night during the festive season because phantom foxes can be seen and their weird barking heard during the night. Nothing would persuade the locals to venture near these so-called 'man-killing foxes'.

George Templer of Stover Park, the builder of the famous Granite Railway, was a keen huntsman who kept a pack of his own hounds. There was one fox, however, which always eluded the hounds although they chased it repeatedly. Eventually it died of old age but at times its ghost appears on the wall outside Stover, now a school. There was actually a report in the local paper of a man having an accident in his car when he had to swerve to avoid a fox which had jumped off the wall on to the bonnet of his car and then simply vanished into thin air. He is not the only person to have reported such an incident.

Ghostly horses are usually seen in the company of human ghosts. They are either the trusty steeds of highwaymen, or else they are pulling carriages in which sits a human ghost. For instance, the well-known horses that draw along Lady Howard, ex wife of four husbands, are of jet black. In the dead of night the coach is heard rattling through the streets of Tavistock on its way to the moor and at other times the Lady is doing penance, running in front of the coach and four in the form of a hound with red flashing eyes.

At Ipplepen near Newton Abbot, Sam Richards, the folk singer, spoke of a herd of white horses, which gallop through the village, again in the middle of the night, rush onto Dartmoor and hurl themselves from a high rock. No one knows where they come from or why they do this.

There are not many accounts of ghostly cats, domestic as opposed to the famous big cats. In Prince's *Worthies of Devon* there is a story, which took place in the days of King Edward II. John Powderham, a tanner's son, announced he was the true Edward, son of Edward I, saying a nurse had changed him in his cradle. As he was about to be hanged for treason and forgery, however, he changed his story and confessed he had been persuaded to tell this falsehood by the familiar spirit which lived in his house, in the likeness of a cat, and had three years earlier assured him that he should by rights be King of England!

As in life, these ghostly creatures can be a comfort or a nuisance. Most of the animals I have written about here have stories attached to them, which give their 'existence' some justification, unlike the big cats, which seem to be more random in making their appearances. There is no question, however, that ghostly creatures of some description do wander the Devon countryside and you can never be sure whether the rustling of leaves from behind the hedgerow in the lane is caused by the wind or by a mysterious creature stealthily watching your every move.

13

Not All the Spirits Are on the Optic

Pubs and inns can be a source of ghostly happenings, as the buildings are often centuries old and have a colourful history of visitors, from royalty to brigands and highwaymen. Some even have a ghost in residence before being converted into a hostelry, as is the case at the Black Dog inn at Uplyme. They say a dog is man's best friend, well that would certainly be true of the large black ghost dog which features in this story, first written up in 1866 by Larwood and Hotten in their *History of Signboards*.

It seems a farmer lived in a cottage where, every night, a large black dog would come and sit opposite him in the chimney corner. The farmer's friend told him if he had any sense he'd chase it off but, as it caused him no expense or trouble, he couldn't be bothered.

One night though, his patience snapped. He seized the poker and chased the dog out of the room. Suddenly, it made an upward leap through the ceiling, making a huge hole in the plaster, from which fell a heap of gold and silver coins from the reign of Charles I. The money from the sale of these proved to be enough to buy the cottage opposite and open up the Black Dog.

The dog now started wandering up and down Dog Lane. One woman who saw it described it as 'getting bigger and bigger 'til he was high as the trees by the wayside', he then turned into a cloud and vanished.

Many years ago, Theo Brown visited the pub and talked to the owners who said they had not seen the dog but met many people who had. Apparently it crosses the boundary between Devon and Dorset every night, rattling the loose chain attached to its collar.

In 1959, during the holiday season, a young couple and their son booked into the pub for the night. After dinner, they went for a walk down the lane, which is bordered by hedges on both sides. Out of one of these appeared a black dog at eye level; it floated in front of them into the hedge opposite and simply vanished. It is said that anyone who sees this apparition will die within the year, though it seems nothing happened to this particular family.

Perhaps one of the most unusual 'pub haunts' is a monolith at the Oxenham Arms at South Zeal. The monolith stands in the wall of a small bar behind the main one and the monks built the original house around it. It is said to date back more than 5,000 years, and however deeply people have excavated, they have never reached the base. Consequently down the years it has become looked upon as 'supernatural'.

The Coombe Cellars pub is said to be the most haunted in Devon. This particular inn on the River Teign was once called The Smugglers because it was the headquarters for this ancient practice of illegal trading.

In 1968 the barmaid, Margaret Marshall, slept in a bedroom above the bar and suffered the most terrible nightmares, which centred on the fact that she was being strangled. She was certain that someone or thing, which had in the past been involved in a violent scene, haunted her bedroom.

No one took her seriously, however, until the owner, Jim Harvey, went to a local sale with the intention of buying anything that had a connection with the pub, and which might be of interest to visitors. He bought some odd bits and pieces but nothing of particular value. It was when he was sorting out his purchases back at the pub that he took particular notice of a painting of a woman. Peering closer at the figures depicted he saw she lay half naked on a bed and a man in a mask was bending over her with his hands around her neck, clearly about to strangle her.

When Margaret saw the picture she let out a scream, shouting, 'That's my room. Look! The walls are still painted that awful

The Coombe Cellars, reputed to be the most haunted pub in the county

green, there's even some of the old pieces of furniture and the window is in the same position, near the door ... oh my God!'

When the first shock had subsided, Jim got a local historian to have a look at the picture. He said by the clothes the man was wearing and the furniture it probably depicted the room as it had been about 100 years ago. The window was open and evidently the man had climbed in, aroused the sleeping girl and realising she would be able to identify him, strangled her. Without doubt it was the room in which Margaret slept. The signature of the artist was on the back with the title 'Death at the Inn'. Eventually old records proved the painter had once stayed at the inn.

The former doubters had to apologise to Margaret and the picture was hung in the bar. She never had the dream again, so perhaps the ghost had been laid to rest once it had been acknowledged! Many people said they had felt an evil influence in that particular bedroom, however, and no one wanted to sleep there.

Not surprisingly, monks, well known for their love of the amber nectar, make frequent ghostly appearances in pubs. The most famous of these is Freddie at the Pig and Whistle at Littlehempston. He was a randy French monk who resided at Buckfast Abbey about 400 years ago and used to ride six miles to the pub to visit his lady friend of easy virtue! He always entered by the same door, now a window, which, although tightly fastened, frequently swings open.

Freddie was a wily bird for when he was dallying with his lady if he heard someone approaching he would escape into a tunnel which led from the inn to a nearby chapel and be found telling his beads.

There is no reason to suppose Freddie is a particularly friendly ghost. Some years ago when I first visited the pub, two of the dogs, who belonged to the owners, had died quite suddenly. One of them had dashed out of the front door into the road in front of a car, although it had never before used the main entrance in all the months they had been there. The other one simply dropped dead, although he had no illness and the vet, after carrying out a post mortem, could offer no cause of death. In addition, bottles would explode, workmen refused to stay on the premises and taps which were not connected to any pipe were found running.

Once someone was even foolish enough to mock the story of Freddie. When he left the pub later he crashed his car a few yards up the road and said he had had to swerve to miss some silly old fool, dressed like a monk, who seemed to disappear when the man got out of his vehicle. When a chair was kept near the bar, known as Freddie's chair, all dogs would steer clear of it with hackles raised.

Built for monks, the Monks Retreat at Broadhempston has a rather unusual and quite harmless haunt in the form of a smell. On reading Chips Barber's fascinating book *Haunted Pubs in Devon*, he says that he distinguished the aroma at once. He recognised it immediately as incense and goes on to say: 'It was most commonly noticed in the pub at Easter or other religious dates.'

At the Old Inn at Widecombe, a young girl can be heard crying in one of the bedrooms. One theory is given me by a local that this is the ghost of Kitty Jay whose grave is at Hound Tor, and she

The Old Inn, Widecombe

is said to be crying for her lost baby, although what she is doing in the pub is not specified.

She was a 15-year-old kitchen maid, an orphan apprentice from the Newton Abbot Workhouse, who hanged herself in a barn at the farm near Manaton, where she worked. Her employer's son had made her pregnant, a highly unacceptable state of affairs, which led to her taking her own life. Suicides were not granted the luxury of a known grave in consecrated ground, so she was buried where three parishes meet in order that not one parish could be deemed responsible.

The other haunt at the Old Inn is Harry, who spends much of his time disappearing through a solid wall into the kitchen. Why he does this, nobody knows, maybe he just appreciates good food.

A close friend once worked as receptionist at the Royal Castle, Dartmouth and she told me the story of the sound of a coach and horses, which is heard but not seen on what was once the cobbled floor of a yard in front of the hotel and is now the reception area.

It seems that Princess Mary of Orange, wife of William, who was to become King of England, did not care for storms at sea. A few days before William and his queen were due to travel to England, the weather was fine and she decided to take advantage of this, leaving in advance of her husband in case the weather should change during the treacherous autumn days. Consequently she arrived in Dartmouth several days before William who, when he set sail, encountered a fierce storm blowing up channel so had to land at Brixham.

The king sent over a messenger to tell the princess and her ladies to make ready for he was sending a coach, which was to bring her to join him. The coach duly arrived at 2 am, clattering into the yard, as it periodically still does today in ghostly form, preceded a little while before by the galloping horseman. Carriage doors are opened and shut, wheels rumble over cobbles and the clock strikes 2 am. The coach has made its ghostly journey once more. As a result, some of the staff have been known to leave because their nerves cannot stand the racket.

The Who'd Have Thought It pub at Milton Combe, near Yelverton is apparently so named because of the landlord getting some kind of shock or unwelcome surprise. History does not relate if it was an increase in the price of beer, the window tax or some other well thought up charge by the powers that be, whatever it was he was not happy about it. The ghost here is not a monk but a Cavalier who is said to have the most beautiful ringlets but rather mournful eyes. If you are staying there he may sit on the end of your bed, simply gazing at you, which I feel could be rather off-putting under some circumstances. One of the landlords of this pub had the delightful name of Abe Beer and he is said to return, to see that his old hostelry is being properly run.

Another landlord who is also said to return in ghostly form for the same reason is at the Nobody Inn at Doddiscombsleigh. The inn dates back to the 1500s and the story here is that when the landlord died his body disappeared from the coffin. He was apparently so fond of the pub that he needed the body to haunt the premises to make sure it was well run!

Finally we have another Cavalier, Sydney Godolphin, a poet, elected Member of Parliament at the age of 18 and a close friend of Ben Johnson. He was just 30 when, fighting for the King, he was seriously wounded in a skirmish against the Parliamentarians. He was carried to the porch of the lovely mullioned and gabled inn, the Three Crowns in Chagford, where he died. His footsteps are often heard in the inn and some claim to have seen him walking through walls, a particularly favourite trick.

The list of haunted pubs seems almost endless and surely there is no better place to sit and listen to all the wonderful stories, rich in history, of these colourful characters and perhaps raise a glass or two to the ghostly inhabitants of our wayside inns.

14

The Parson and the Clerk

The story of the Parson and Clerk, goes back to the time when a now long forgotten Bishop of Exeter lay dying in the town of Dawlish. The story is brought to mind by a headline in the *Western Morning News*, 'Rocks that inspired legend to vanish?'

It went on: 'Erosion looks like deciding the fate of a landmark, a seaside cliff formation telling the ghostly story of a rock formation near Teignmouth, strange cliff top shapes, which overlook part of the coast and, which are crumbling into the sea.'

When travelling from Paddington to Newton Abbot, I always try to get a seat on the left side of the carriage so I can get a good view of this phenomenon. In the late afternoon the mud flats of the estuary are often turned into a white sheen by the sun as seabirds pick at juicy pieces abounding in the area. Looking backwards through the window after passing the station at Dawlish you can see the rocks much resembling the figures of two people. They are known as the famous Parson and Clerk and now a large piece of the red sandstone has been eroded.

The story goes that, as the aforementioned bishop lay dying, a local parson and his clerk decided to take the long trek to visit him. Local gossip had it that the parson, one of many contenders to succeed the bishop, was eagerly awaiting the man's death in the hope of occupying his place in the cathedral. It seems these two figures were extremely sinister and the parson determined to gain good favour by visiting the ailing churchman.

It was the clerk who usually led the way to Dawlish and he was generally thought to be most reliable and accurate in his navigation, but on this particular night a horrific storm blew up. The pair had spent the day collecting tithes from the local farms, so their thoughts were more occupied with money than with their current predicament.

Suddenly, they realised they had lost their way. The parson practically exploded with rage and discomfort shouting at the clerk, 'A curse upon this desolate upland. I am wet to the skin and shivering with cold. This trackless country is fit for neither man nor beast.' The clerk agreed, he was not a courageous man.

'You fool, Old Nick himself could have done a better job than you,' the parson retorted.

As he spoke lightning split the sky, illuminating the surrounding landscape. They could see a peasant, much like the ones from whom they had been collecting money, riding a moorland pony. 'I see you gentlemen are lost,' his tone was ingratiating and humble. 'In which direction are you heading?'

'To Dawlish. We are in a great hurry and will make it worth your while to get us there,' the parson explained, frightened in case the bishop should die and he not be present.

'As it happens my humble abode is just outside that town and I should be delighted if you would accept my hospitality,' the man replied. 'Stay close or you may be lost again.'

Slowly the threesome made its way. Sometimes the parson thought the storm was weakening and perhaps they could find their own way, but as soon as he looked away from their guide the wind and rain seemed to increase in fury.

At length, they reached the outskirts of Dawlish, coming to an old and dilapidated house. In spite of its appearance, the parson's mouth started to water at the thought of spiced cider and bread and cheese but to his amazement, as they drew near, sounds of laughter and general merriment came from the house. The peasant said with a touch of irony, 'Welcome to my humble abode, I would be honoured if you join me in a bite of supper before you proceed.'

The invitation was too tempting to refuse. As they dismounted a hooded figure appeared, to lead away their horses. For some reason the parson shivered as an eerie feeling spread though him, however the peasant beckoned them to the open door.

Once inside, they saw the tables were covered with meats and puddings, pies and kegs of ale and cider. Suddenly, the clerk recognised the guests as people they used to know who had since died. He tried to warn the priest but he was far too engaged with singing and drinking to notice.

Finally, as dawn broke, a messenger came to say the bishop had died. The parson was overjoyed although he was reluctant to leave his new friends to return to the elements. The clerk had fallen asleep and begged to be left by the fire, but greed for the honour of position had overtaken the desire of the parson for food and drink. They donned their coats and wished their companions farewell, thanking their host warmly for his generous hospitality, while their horses were brought to the door. The man replied, 'It is perhaps I that should be thanking you, we shall meet again no doubt.'

At first their horses would not move but by means of spurs and whips they managed to make the animals move at last. As they rode, the parson glanced back at the strange mansion from which they had just come. To his horror it had turned into a pile of jagged rocks and the air was now filled with screams and chilling laughter. Their earlier drinking companions had turned into mad demons, dancing and leaping about the horses. Their peasant guide was the most horrific looking of all as he cackled with manic laughter. Mad with terror, the horses ran straight towards the direction of the cliffs with the man at their heels, the riders powerless to stop them as they dashed through the dark miles.

Eventually, the maddened beasts plunged over the cliffs into the raging sea below, the two men clinging to them for dear life.

By sunrise the storm had vanished, the sea calm as a millpond.

Two horses were later found wandering quietly along the sands but of human bodies there was no sign, just two gaunt rocks that had mysteriously appeared overnight below the cliffs. Because of the way they had suddenly materialised and their size and shape they were inevitably known as the Parson and Clerk.

As I write, it seems they too are doomed by erosion, leaving no trace of the greedy parson who waited so eagerly for a dead man's shoes, an ironic ending to such a story.

15

The Curse of the Evil Eye

Most people today still think of witches, if not with tall hats and broomsticks, certainly as of the black variety. Many witches, however, are white and do nothing but good; in fact, white witches are often healers. Certainly in the old days they studied the weather, practised healing with herbs and were held in great awe by their innocent neighbours.

Nowadays, white witches in Devon are ordinary people who happen to have some kind of mysterious power and use these natural gifts for healing and blessing. One unusual example of a person with the gift for healing is John Goodman from the South Hams, an ex Group Captain, who flew Wellingtons and Mosquitoes during the Second World War. He was as practical and down to earth as anyone can be and yet he found he could suddenly heal people by a laying on of hands. This power manifested itself shortly after a mysterious light appeared on the cross in the church of which he was a churchwarden. When I met John, I was suffering with a bad back and I have to admit that when he held his hands at some distance from the area of the pain, it vanished and I felt a great warmth. I never asked him if he felt like a white witch or sorcerer but if I had I am sure he would have thrown back his head and roared with laughter. In the Middle Ages of course he would have been considered such a one, although, strangely enough, I don't think we often hear of the male sex in mediaeval times practising witchcraft.

To go back to the past, Dr Gidley of Cullompton wrote in the *Transactions of the Devonshire Assoc (vol 49, pp 69–71)* saying how he came into contact with white witchcraft in 1897. A woman had come to him with a cancerous growth in the breast for which he advised an operation. She then met someone, however, who told her: 'A certain person is ill wishing you, but I can cure your illness'.

The cure called for a sheep's heart to have pins inserted into it at midnight, whilst reciting a formula. The heart then had to be left in the chimney on the bar that holds up the pot hooks. Shortly after this had been carried out a woman neighbour of the cancer victim became weak and feeble. Her condition and death synchronized exactly with the diminishing and disappearance of the growth in the other woman's breast. In fact, she lived for a further ten years with no sign of a recurrence.

As a postscript to this story, some years ago, while talking to my wonderful informant of tales of the supernatural, Algy May of Rowbrook Farm, he told me that Canon Hall who lived at Leusdon saw a piece of liver hanging in the recess of a hearth at a farm near where he lived. This had pins stuck in it, just as in the case of the cancer victim, and the liver was still quite fresh. This occurred in the 20th century!

Surely this idea and feel for witchcraft would not have survived if there weren't at least something in it. How often do we see a natural force for good come first, only to be confirmed later in the lab, such as carrots being good for the eyesight or the old wives' cure of hot chicken soup to relieve a mucous condition that really works.

Any witches reading this who have not kept up with current affairs will be relieved to know that being a witch ceased to be a capital offence in 1735. From then on it became a private matter to be dealt with by supposed victims, but in 1924 a farmer called Matthews from Clyst St Lawrence was sent to prison for maliciously wounding his neighbour who he alleged had ill-wished his pig, by using a crystal.

In *Devonshire Characters*, Sabine Baring Gould tells of an old woman who was a white witch and received presents from all the farmers in the district to keep her sweet. Meeting a child from school she would 'hold her with her eye' and say, 'My chiel I knows one like you, red cheeks, black hair, 'er shrivelled up, cheeks grew white and she just died ...' Before the day was out a chicken or batch of eggs arrived at the witch's cottage as a present from the child's mother. This tactic gives a fine example of the considerable influence witches could exert over their neighbours, and maybe this particular witch was only 'white' because she was constantly plied with gifts.

The curse of the evil eye, or the holding of other humans by looking at them intently for a few minutes, which the white witch exerted over the child, can have extremely harmful effects. Bet Webb, known as the witch of Dartmoor, lived at Postbridge. On one occasion the local driver of a carriage, who used to take people to Widecombe, incurred her displeasure. The evil eye was at once turned on him and she prophesied he would meet trouble before the end of his journey. He ignored the threat and forgot all about it but nearing Runnage an effectual stop was put to the journey when one of the wheels came off and the carriage fell apart beyond repair.

In 1896 a man in Sourton was committed for trial at Okehampton for sheep stealing, for which penalties ranged from deportation to hanging. The prisoner's wife, who was a witch, jumped up in court and shouted at the magistrate, 'You black nosed old devil, you'll be dead in a week and nobody connected with this case shall die in his bed'.

Within a week, the chairman of the magistrates dropped dead in a field as he was talking to his farm bailiff, another magistrate committed suicide and the farmer who had prosecuted the witch's husband knocked over a lamp and was burned to death. Later the clerk to the magistrates fell dead whilst riding his bicycle as he was cycling near Okehampton. The cause of death was never discovered.

In 1929, when witchcraft was considered a thing of the past, a gipsy with the usual basket of oddments called at a farmhouse near South Molton. The farmer's daughter refused to buy anything. The woman asked for a glass of cider but the girl refused. Then milk was requested and also refused, until eventually, begrudgingly, the girl gave the gipsy a glass of water. She immediately poured it on the ground muttering a few words as she did so. Returning the empty glass to the girl, she left.

The girl told her neighbour, who said some ill luck was obviously intended. She repeated the story to a gipsy friend, who said, 'That is the worst gipsy curse of all'.

The girl was engaged to be married. A house and furniture had been bought, the wedding day fixed, and the banns were called the next Sunday for the first time. As the words 'if any should know of just cause … etc' were spoken by the priest, the bridegroom dropped dead beside his prospective bride.

The power of the evil eye even extends to animals, for instance a sheepdog can hold sheep with its eyes. A woman took my grandmother to court once, because she said my grandmother's red setter dog had 'held' her with his eyes in the lane outside gran's house and so terrified her she had a miscarriage. Was this witchcraft?

As I have mentioned in an earlier chapter, it was widely believed that witches could transform themselves into hares. There is an old story of a couple who lived at Folly Gate near Hatherleigh and while the old man was out shooting rabbits, a hare jumped up from the grass. He took aim but at the last moment thought better of it. Getting home he laughingly told his wife of it saying he could not understand why he had hesitated. She replied, 'Twas just as well, for I was the hare'.

Another witch called Hannah Henley was frequently chased as a hare by the Cotley Harriers and in 1885 a man at Rose Ash, near South Molton, shot a hare with a bullet made from a sixpence. The same day, a local woman suspected of being a witch was found with wounds in her leg.

Crossing is another writer with many tales of witches' tricks, including the use of the knotted cord designed to inflict injury. The witch would tie a number of knots in a cord and over the first one utter some charm whilst blowing on it, and the victim would begin to feel the ill effects of the enchantment. On the following day the charm was repeated over the second knot and the victim would grow worse, and so on until the last knot was reached when the illness would prove fatal.

In front of the Hunter's Lodge Inn, between Honiton and Ottery, is a great stone on which witches used to sacrifice their victims. On certain nights, so the macabre story goes, it is said the stone rolls down to the river to cleanse itself, lubricated by the blood that had been shed on it!

If you are beginning to feel nervous about the state of witchcraft in Devon, Sarah Hewett the well known writer on such affairs, describes an old Devon counter measure which can be employed against witches and their evil powers. Take three small necked stone jars; place in each the liver of a frog, stuck full of new pins, and the heart of a toad, stuck full of thorns from a holy thorn bush. Cork and seal each jar. Bury them in three different churchyards seven inches from the surface and seven feet from the porch. While in the act of burying each, repeat the Lord's Prayer backwards. As the hearts and livers decay, so will the witch's power vanish.

Quite possibly so will you, if well meaning friends have seen you performing these rites and have you removed somewhere for your personal safety!

16

Haunts of the Highways

If you are of a nervous disposition, there are two particular roads in Devon you would do well to avoid, especially if you are on your own and it is dark.

My first grizzly tale is from an account by R. Thurston Hopkins in his book *Literary Landmarks of Devon and Cornwall*, published in 1926. In one chapter he describes how he was in a pub, called the Dolphin Inn in Colyton, chatting with the locals, when for some reason the talk turned to progress, particularly the way in which the car and bus had given a new lease of life to lonely villages, even bringing business to parts of the country which had been almost dead for 300 years.

Someone remarked, 'Motors didn't do much good for Bob Levett,' and out came the story of this man who, in the early 1900s, had been run over on the road near Gatcombe Chase.

Levett was hit violently by a car, which must have been travelling at a great speed, and disappeared equally quickly. The friends who found Bob carried him into the Dolphin. He was covered in blood and spattered from head to foot with the paint from the tin he had been carrying.

He died in the pub almost immediately and the driver of the car was never found. There were rumours about someone called Plashett, a bit of an inventor, who owned a garage at Musbury. It seemed he knew a lot more about the accident than he let on, he did say however, that a Major Cheyney had driven his big German car into the garage about half an hour after the time of the accident. The car had a dented wing, which was spattered with the same colour paint with which Bob had been covered. Nothing was proved, however, and everyone seemed very anxious not to make any enquiries.

It transpired that Major Cheyney was subsequently killed during the war and young Plashett crashed when he was piloting a plane.

It was at this point in the conversation that one of the group, Nicholas Apsley, a tall, bearded man aged about 70, dropped his bombshell. 'People here don't like talking about it, 'tis all past and done.' He paused, then added so softly they could hardly hear his words, 'But Bob Levett's been seen since. He waits about on the road between Gatcombe Chase and Colyton where it happened. People see him running and hear him shouting. They say he's looking for the car that killed him, and he can run like the very devil. No car can go fast enough to shake him off. First of all you hear his feet pattering behind you, pattering in the quiet and the dark, then the hiss of his breath right in your ear, then he passes you and goes on ahead out of hearing. You don't never catch up with him.'

There was silence for a moment when he finished, then someone recalled how one night a stranger to the area, who knew nothing about the accident or the ghost, knocked up the landlord of the Dolphin, almost speechless with terror. Something or someone had overtaken him on the road and he was too frightened to drive any further, he could feel it was evil.

Nicholas went on, 'They do say sometimes he doesn't pass you but springs on the car itself. A couple of years ago a car crashed again on that very spot and was smashed to bits. The chap who was driving wasn't actually killed but he went soft in the head, crying out that a man was chasing him, going to strangle him. The doctor they called couldn't pacify him. They found great black bruises like fingermarks on his throat.'

After reading this hair-raising account, I went off to Colyton and here I found things got even more curious. I managed to find an old local, leaning on a gate by the church. I asked him if he could direct me to the pub called the Dolphin. Slowly he took his pipe from his mouth and gave me an odd look. 'Ain't no Dolphin here now, missus, turned into a bank years ago, local pub's called the Kingfisher, down there on the right.'

Well there may have been no Dolphin pub but I was in Dolphin Street. I parked the car and went in through the back door of the Kingfisher. In the narrow, dark passageway I found a small plaque engraved simply with the words 'Dolphin House'. In the bar, where I went in for a drink and a chat, once I mentioned the name Dolphin everyone clammed up. I asked if they remembered anything about the hit and run story and the atmosphere turned distinctly chilly, so I left and made enquiries in other pubs in the area. Unfortunately, I drew a blank.

The next ghost of the highways, the hitchhiker of the A38, has been seen by many people, and perhaps might make you think twice about offering a lift to a stranger.

In 1970, the *Western Morning News* ran a story about a Mrs K. Swithenbank, who was travelling along the road from Oake to Taunton late one evening, when she saw a middle aged man standing in the middle of the road, near the Heatherton Grange Hotel. The figure was wearing a long grey overcoat and shining a torch on the ground as though he were looking for someone or somebody.

She saw him too late and braked so violently she skidded and was sure she must have hit him, although she had felt no impact on the car. Badly shaken at the thought of what she might find she got out of the car. She searched all over the road and in the ditches at the side but there was no sign of anyone, the road was completely deserted. Similar stories were reported to the police but no explanation could be found.

It was my friend and fellow writer Harry Unsworth, sadly no longer with us, who then gave me, and the *Western Morning News*, a full account of the ghostly hitchhiker.

It was the late 1950s and at the time Harry was a long distance lorry driver. One morning at 3 o'clock, he had to draw up quickly to avoid a man who was standing near the Blackbird Inn, a short distance from Heatherton Grange. It was against his policy to give lifts to strangers, and this one certainly looked a bit dodgy, badly in need of a haircut, unshaven and generally scruffy. It was such a terribly stormy wet night, however, that Harry felt he couldn't refuse. The chap looked all in, so he opened the cab door and said, 'Hop in mate.'

To his surprise the man he had taken to be a tramp seemed, from his speech and general attitude, to be well educated. His main topic of conversation, however, turned out to be of the accidents that had happened at this spot. He asked Harry to drop him at Beam Bridge and to be honest Harry was not too sorry in the end to get rid of his rather depressing passenger.

He soon forgot the whole episode. Some weeks later, however, he came across the man in exactly the same spot and in the same foul weather conditions, in fact the whole performance was an exact repeat of the former encounter.

Once more nearly six months passed and in November 1958 there was this man again. This time he was standing on the bridge itself, he asked Harry to wait there while he went back along the road to pick up his bags, which he had left a little way behind. He'd only be 'a couple of ticks' he said.

Harry, rather reluctantly, agreed as he had a strict schedule to keep. Twenty minutes passed but when the man did not return he decided the stranger must have changed his mind and walked away.

After he had driven on about five miles once more he saw the old familiar scene of the torch being waved frantically in front of him. He knew at once it was the same man but it would have been quite impossible for him to have passed Harry and arrive in front of him in the time and no other traffic had passed, so he couldn't have got a lift from someone else.

By now Harry had picked up a considerable speed after the delay and he had to slam on the brakes. The articulated lorry went into a jack-knife skid nearly landing him in the ditch. He leant out of the window swearing, his patience exhausted. As there was no reply he climbed down and walked round afraid he had knocked the man over. He searched the whole area, both sides of the road and even under the lorry. As before, the man and his bags, if he had had them with him, had simply dissolved into thin air.

Not surprisingly, Harry was extremely shaken by this experience and was glad to stop at the next pull-in for some good hot coffee and cheerful human companionship.

The conclusion he had come to was that as it was a well known accident area, this spirit or ghost, for some reason was doomed to try and hitch a lift from the passing traffic forever, either as the victim or the driver who had been involved in some horrific accident.

There is an even more startling sequel to Harry's weird encounter. One morning he noticed a small white Mini parked opposite his house in the cul de sac where he was living at the time. There was a loud knocking at his door and when he opened it two pale faced young men stood on the step. They said they were students from Exeter University and they had read his story in the paper and thought from the description that they recognised a fellow student who had gone missing. They were anxious to trace him and they asked what he was wearing, what he looked like, the colour of his hair and eyes.

They were quite rude, which upset Harry who was the friendliest person, and were insistent for details. When they found he could give them very little help their last remark was, 'Did he talk TO you or THROUGH you?'

Harry said he had no idea what they were talking about and told them to push off, but as he put out his hand to close the door he remembered there had been something about the man's accent that might help. He stepped outside to call after them. The street was completely empty. He had heard no sound of an engine and they would have had to take some seconds to turn the car in the cul de sac and there were quite a few hundred yards to drive to the main road. There was nothing, no car, and no sign of any human being.

So were these visitors and the strange hitchhiker from beyond the grave? We shall never know and neither can I tell you whether the man still haunts that piece of road because I never drive that way. In fact, I have even been known to avoid it by making quite a long detour.

Bibliography

Chips Barber, *Haunted Pubs in Devon*
A. W. Bearne, *Flying Saucers Over the West*
Sabine Baring Gould, *Devonshire Characters*
The Revd Hugh Breton, *The Heart of Dartmoor*
Theo Brown, *Devon Ghosts*
William Crossing, *Guide to Dartmoor*
Elliott O'Donnell, *Haunted Britain*
Dr Gidley, *Transactions of the Devonshire Assoc.* (Vol 49, pp 69–71)
Eric Hemery, *High Dartmoor*
Larwood & Hotten, *History of Signboards*
J. L. Page, *The Rivers of Devon*, 1893
John Prince, *Worthies of Devon*
Ruth St Leger Gordon, *Folklore and Magic of Dartmoor*
R. Thurston Hopkins, *Literary Landmarks of Devon & Cornwall*
Western Morning News
Devon Life

Thanks also to Jack Holman for the Doug Cooper interview.

Index